interloper

fineart nudes & photo-paintings

ricardo acevedo

Photography and prose by Ricardo Acevedo
Layout by Sarajane Helm

First published and printed as a paperback
in the United States of America in September 2011
by PolyMarket Press

ISBN 978-0-9800312-7-0

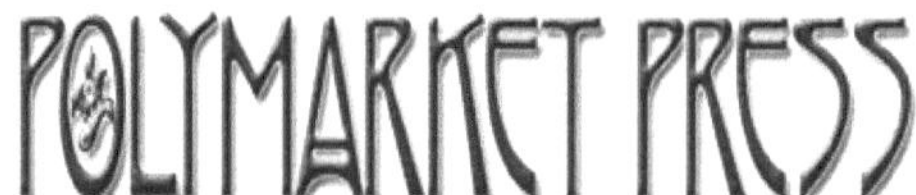

For more information about our books
and the authors and artists who create them,
please visit our web site:

polymarketpress.net

Thank you, you; yes, you...for finding me. I've been lost in my own wilderness for sometime now, waiting for you to come along.

A deep thank you to all the women and men who have given me their heart and soul as model collaborators. By going beyond the obvious you allowed me to be more than just a visual artist. You allowed me to be a storyteller.

Thank you, Sarajane; for embracing human potential.
It embraces you back ten fold.

An emotional thank you to Susan, Violet and Domingo for the blood, sweat, tears and cheers. I love you more than words can define.

Thanks to Robin (Mom) for seeing the diamond in the rough.

And lastly thank you to Gloria Elena & Ben for spending that night together on Foothill Blvd. in Rialto Ca. in the spring of 1959.

Besos... to all

interloper

Up
1995 | B/W chemical photo
O.P.S. - 11" x 17"

A lens to capture the wild let loose
by a gun.
Stealing your source of light
to wither from the lack of sun.

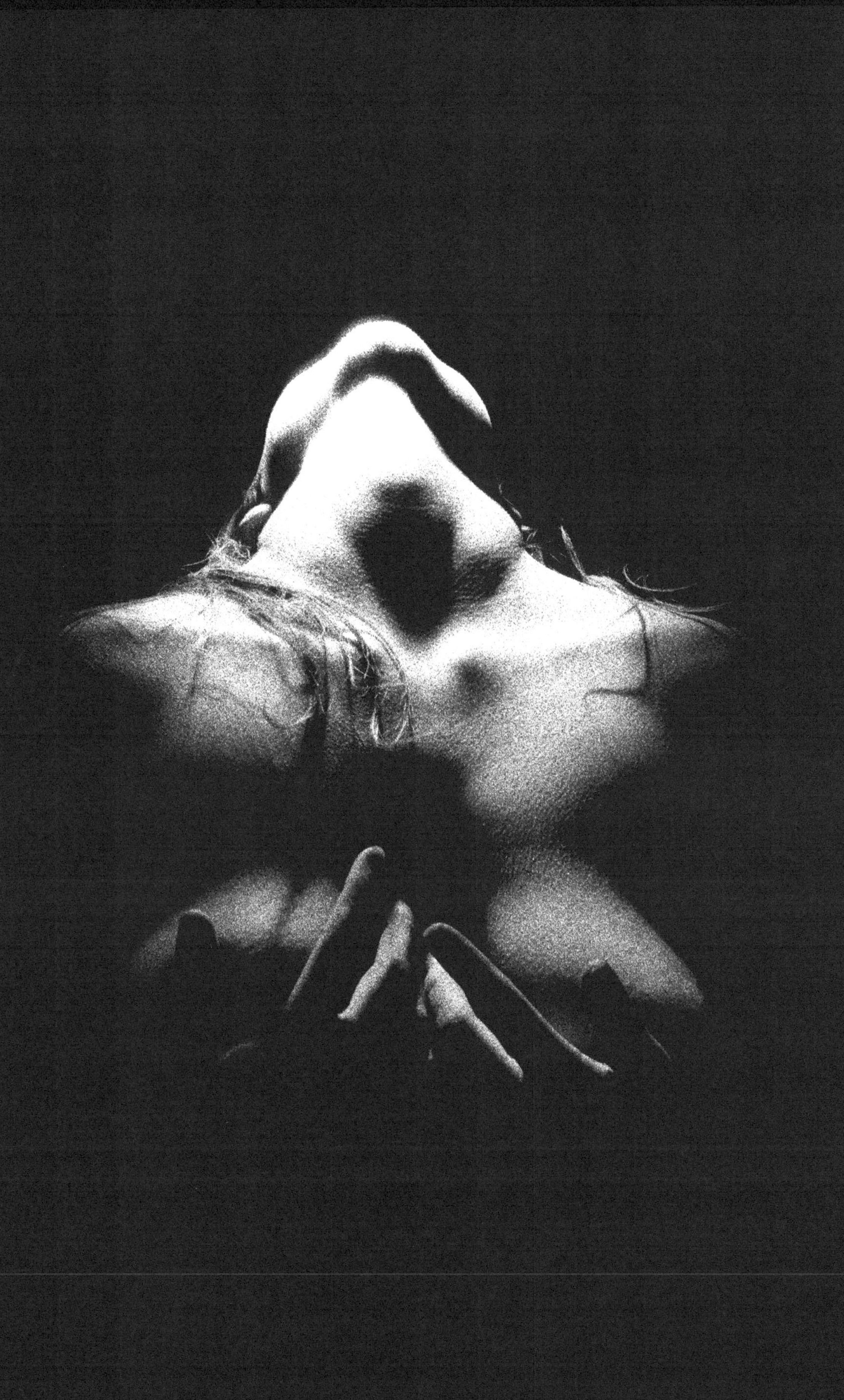

interloper

Light again
1995 | B/W chemical photo
O.P.S. - 11" x 17"

You can't capture them in the wild
They calculate like cheetahs
With broken legs
But can you love a silhouette?
The way you loose it on the world?
No finite features
Only puppetry in black light

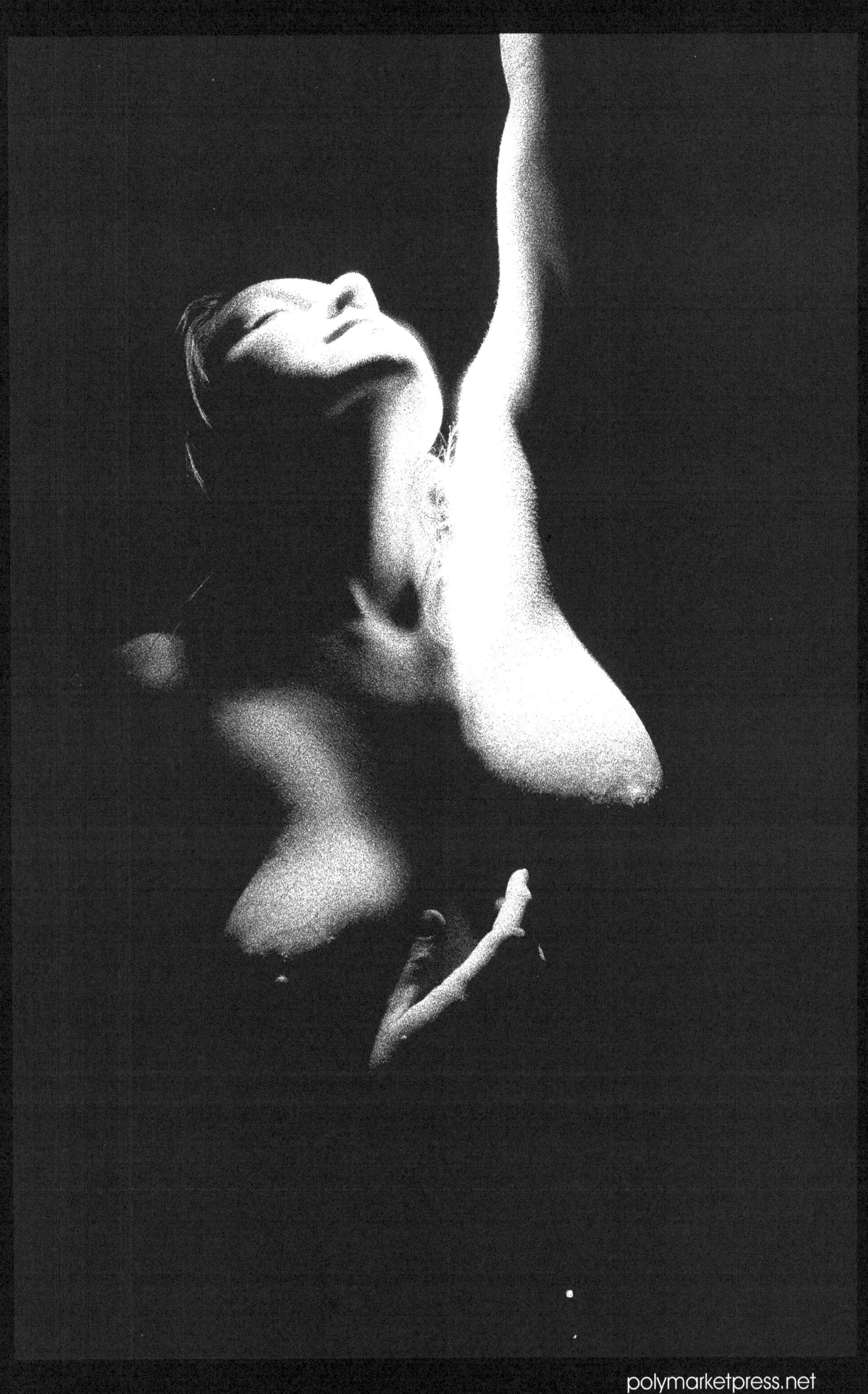

interloper

In here
1995 | B/W chemical photo.
O.P.S. - 11" x 17"

Sometimes they are faceless
Thumping on my chest like hunger pangs
Very smooth heads, no mouth or eyes
But these pressures in my chest have names

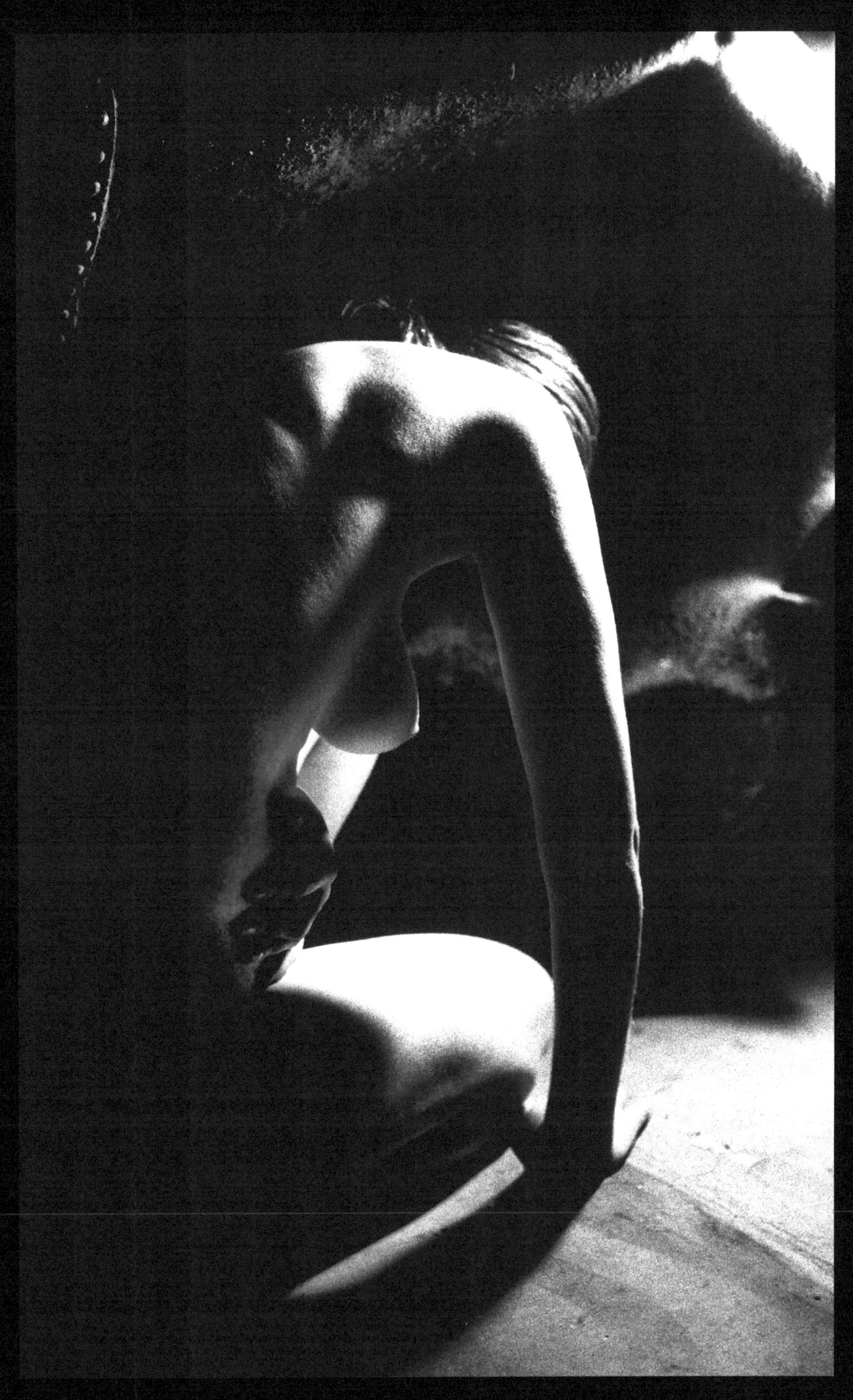

interloper

Beth silhouette
1997 | B/W chemical photo
O.P.S. - 17" x 11"

Fierce light and elongated shadows
Bunnies heat pantomimes bedtime story

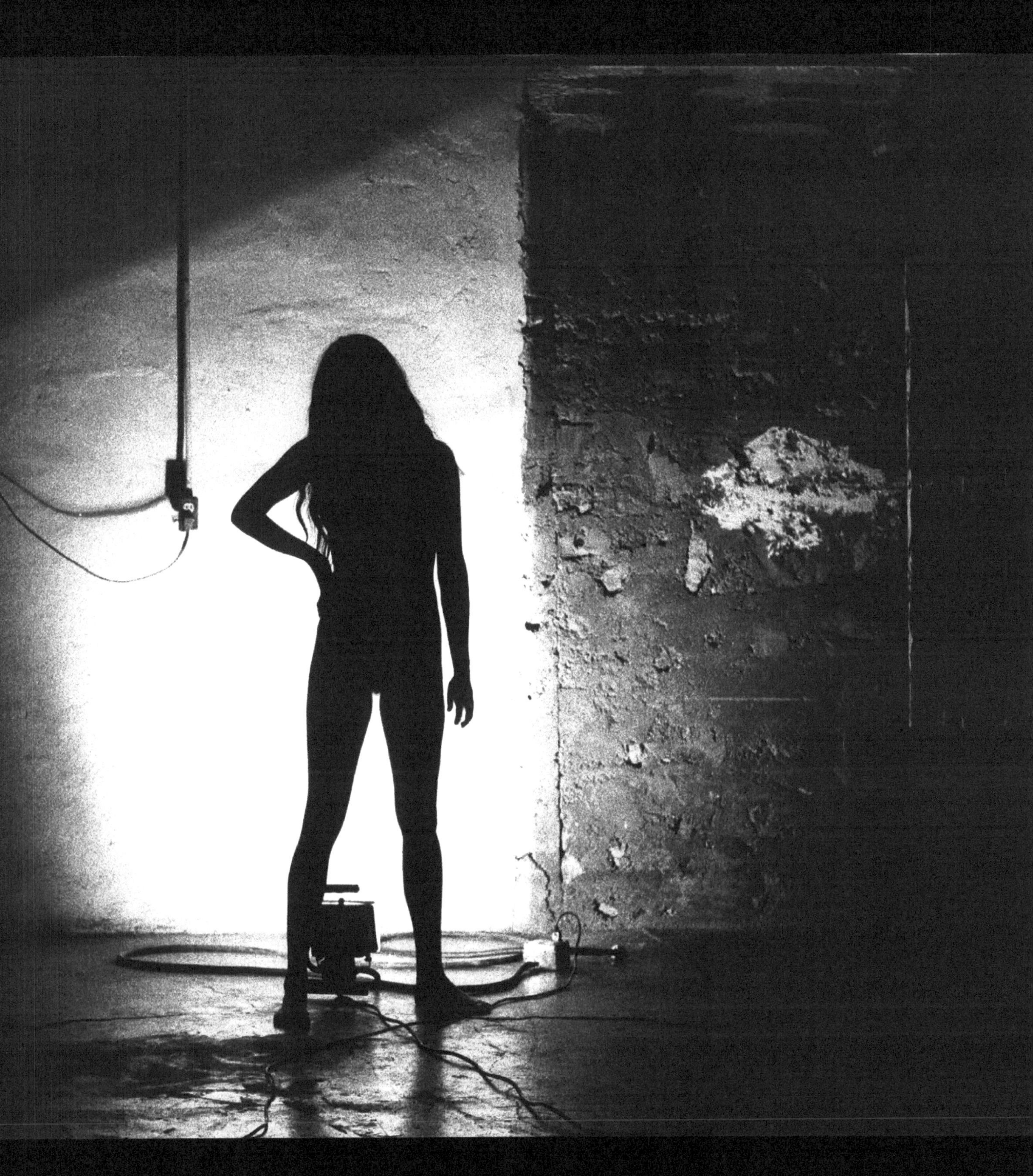

interloper

Lilith
1996 | B/W chemical photo.
O.P.S. - 17" x 11"

It's Dark in here.

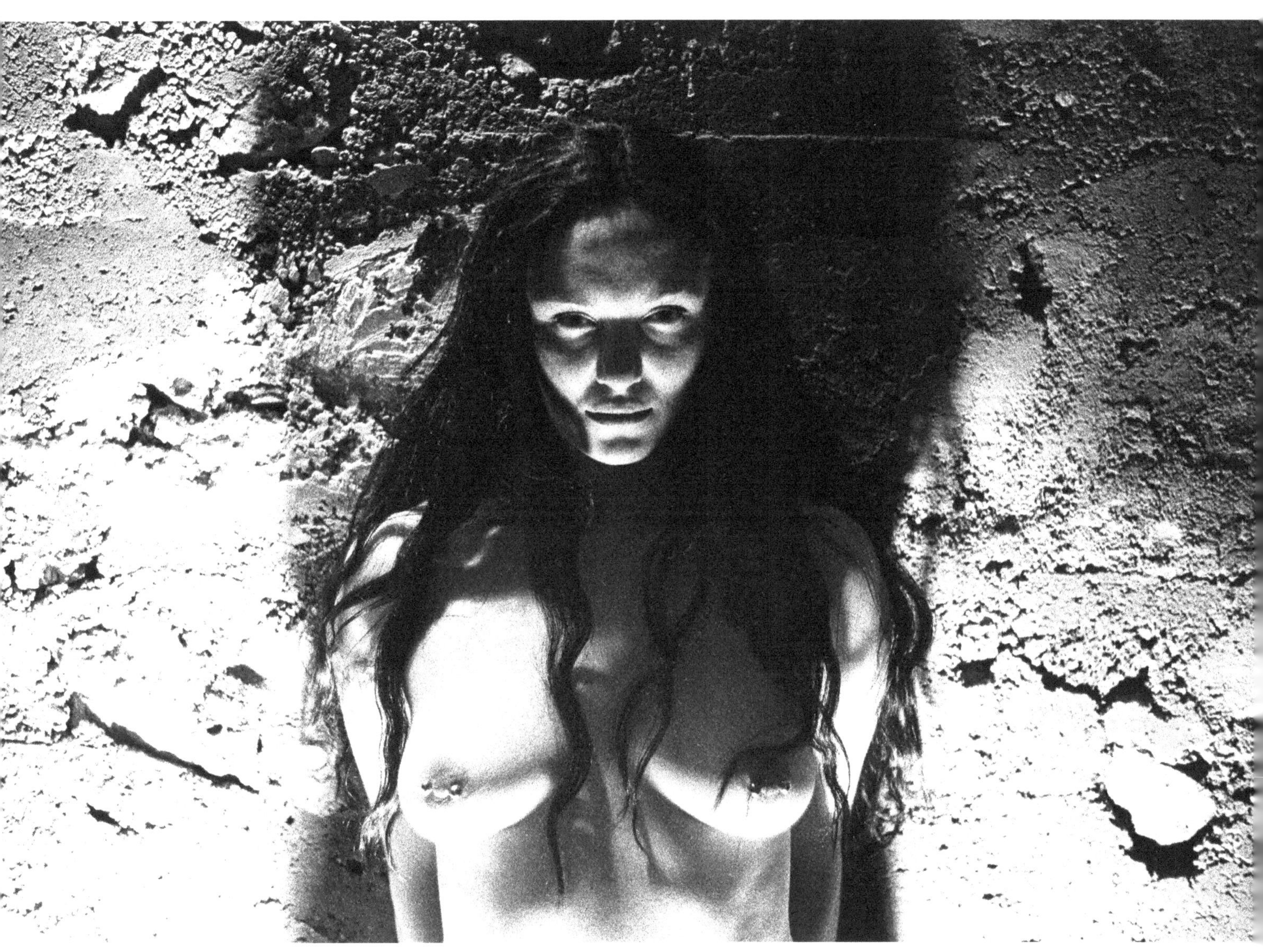

interloper

Bask
1997 | B/W chemical photo
O.P.S. - 17"x 22"

Hand reaching,
Paper's breath,
To inhale thought.
Reclaiming single emotion, on
At a time of
Many shallow pools
Wading souls, need deep
In ecstasy.
Chase, all else blurred
Surrounded by flash
The lightless moment, of
Darkness embraced.

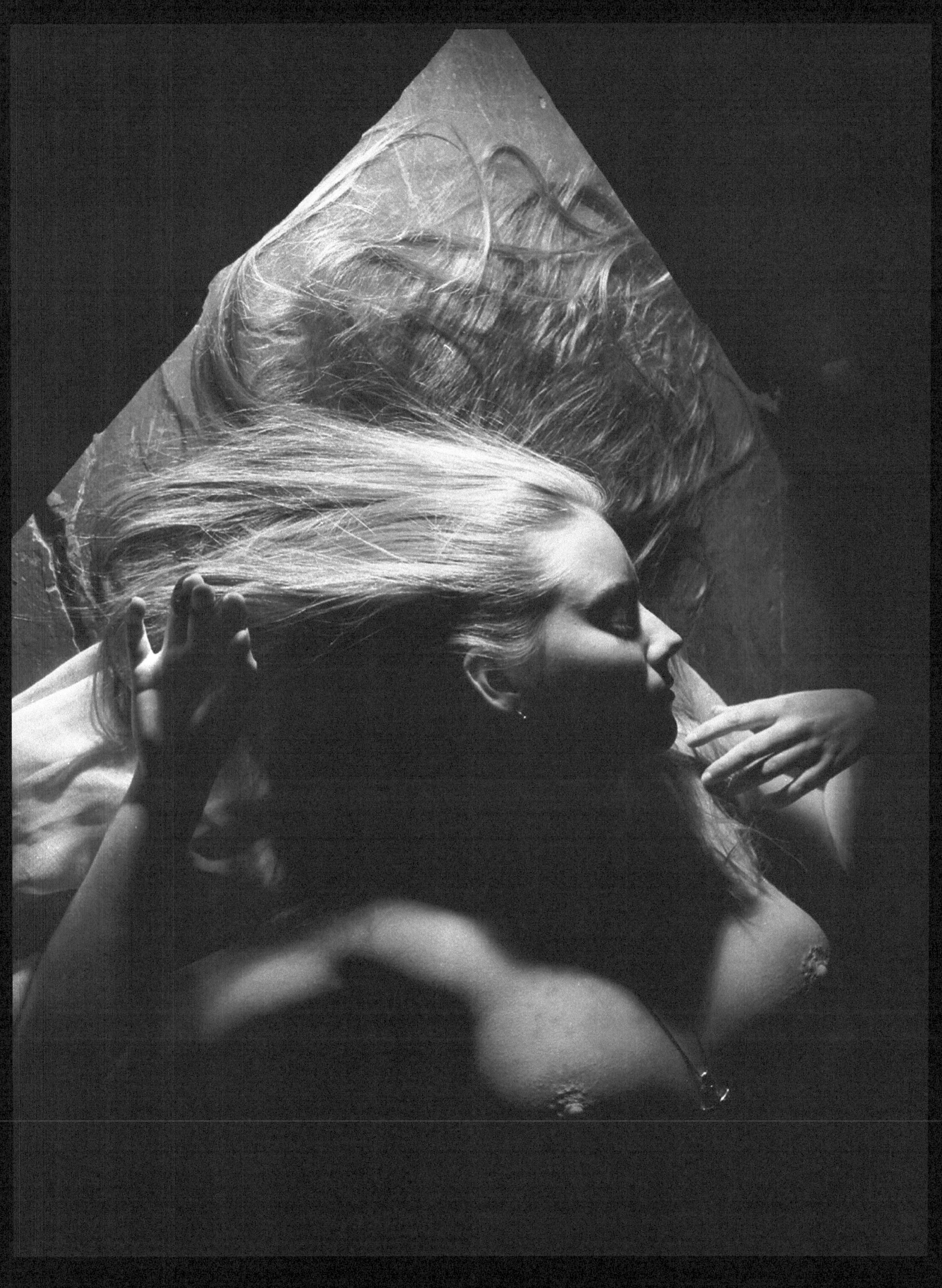

interloper

Ophelia's Lover
2000 | mixed source photo-painting
O.P.S. - 24" x 24"

Perversion opens doors and puts up its gone fishing sign.
That space is filled with shallow breath and the faint aroma of catfish.

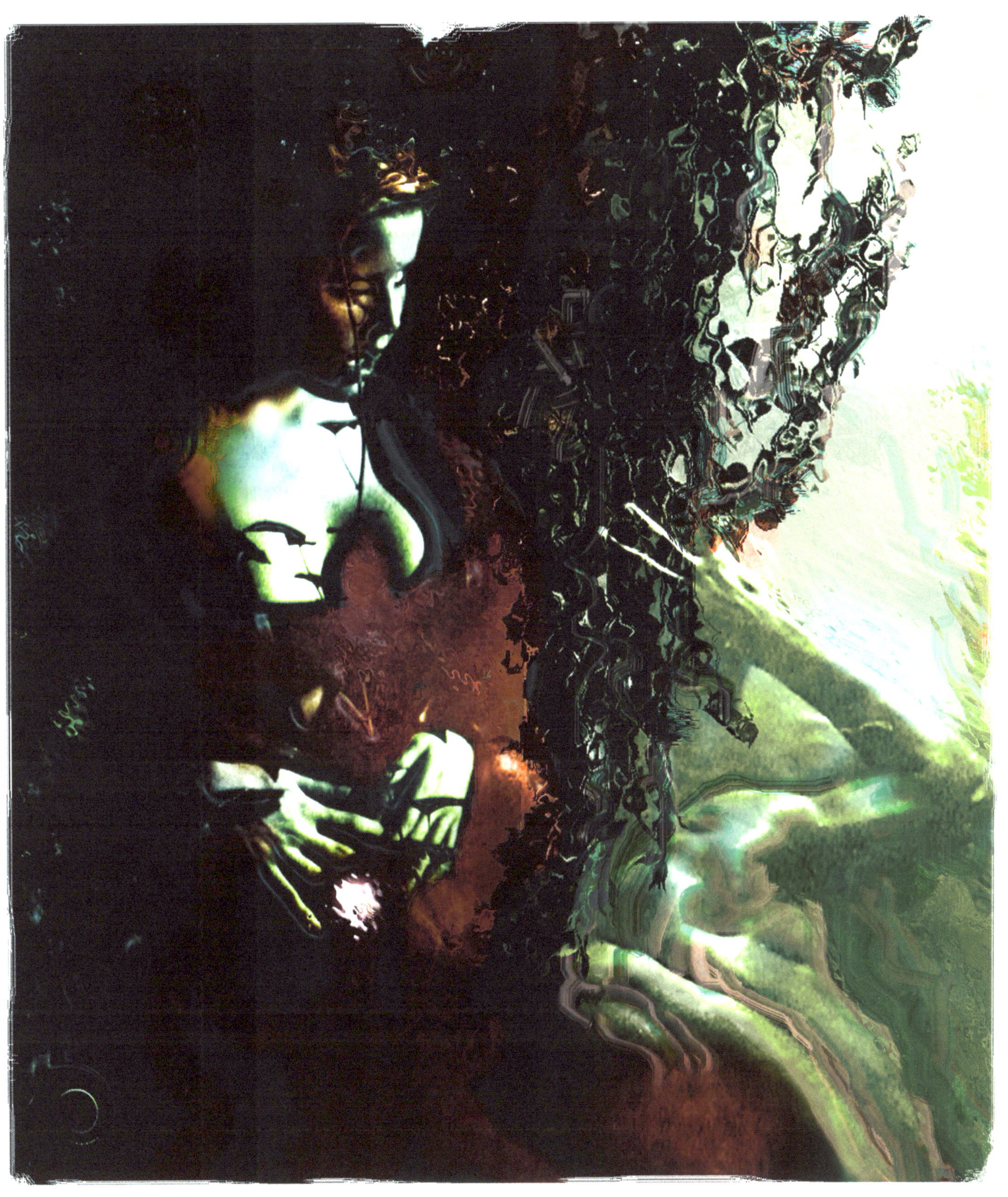

interloper

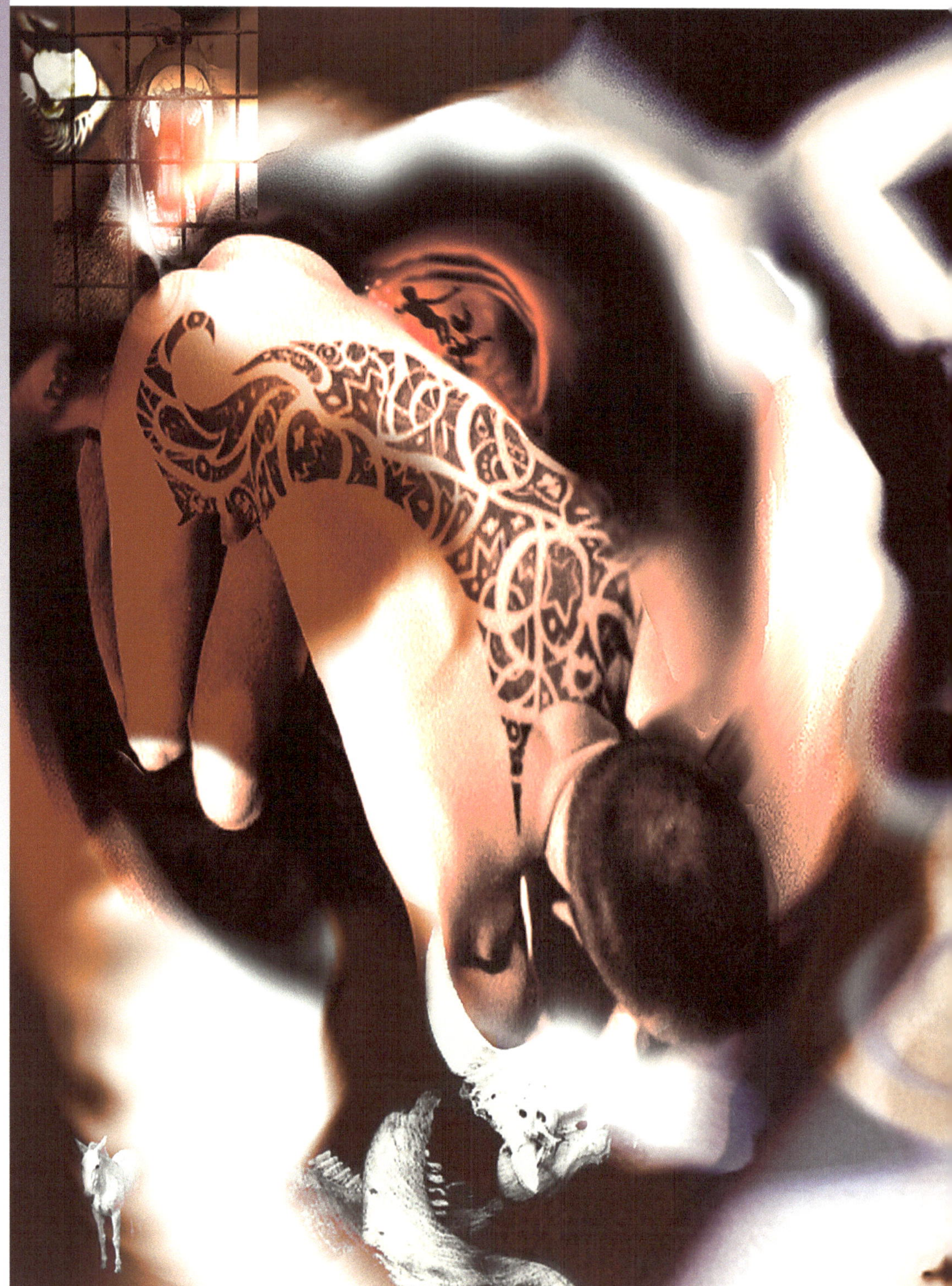

Love vs. Evolution
2000 | mixed source photo-painting
O.P.S - 48″ x 28″

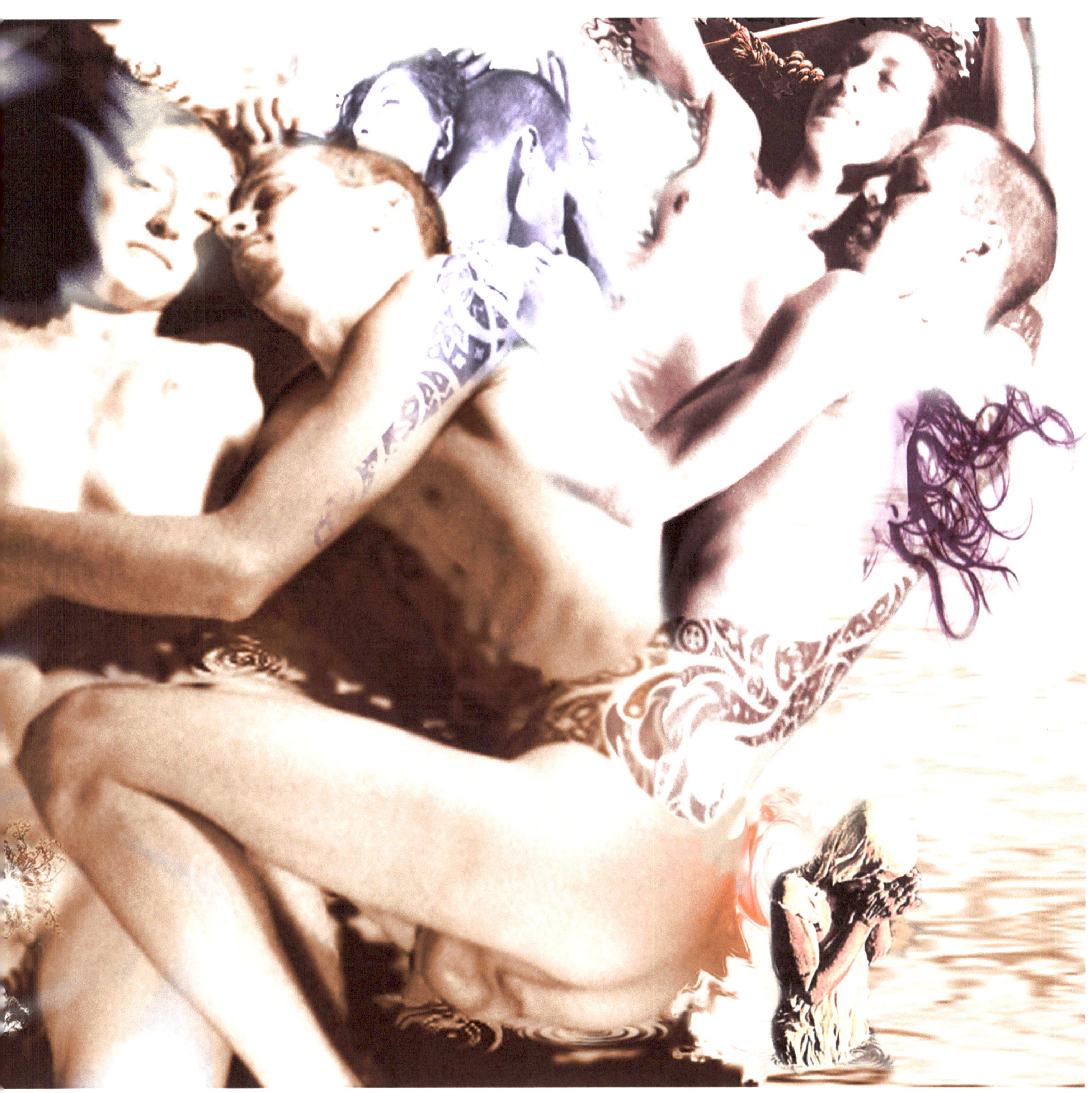

Your cute ellipsis
Your delve of vetch
Overworked fields
Worked hard by
Spark and retch

A lens to capture the wild let loose
By a gun.
Stealing your source of light
To whither from the lack of sun.

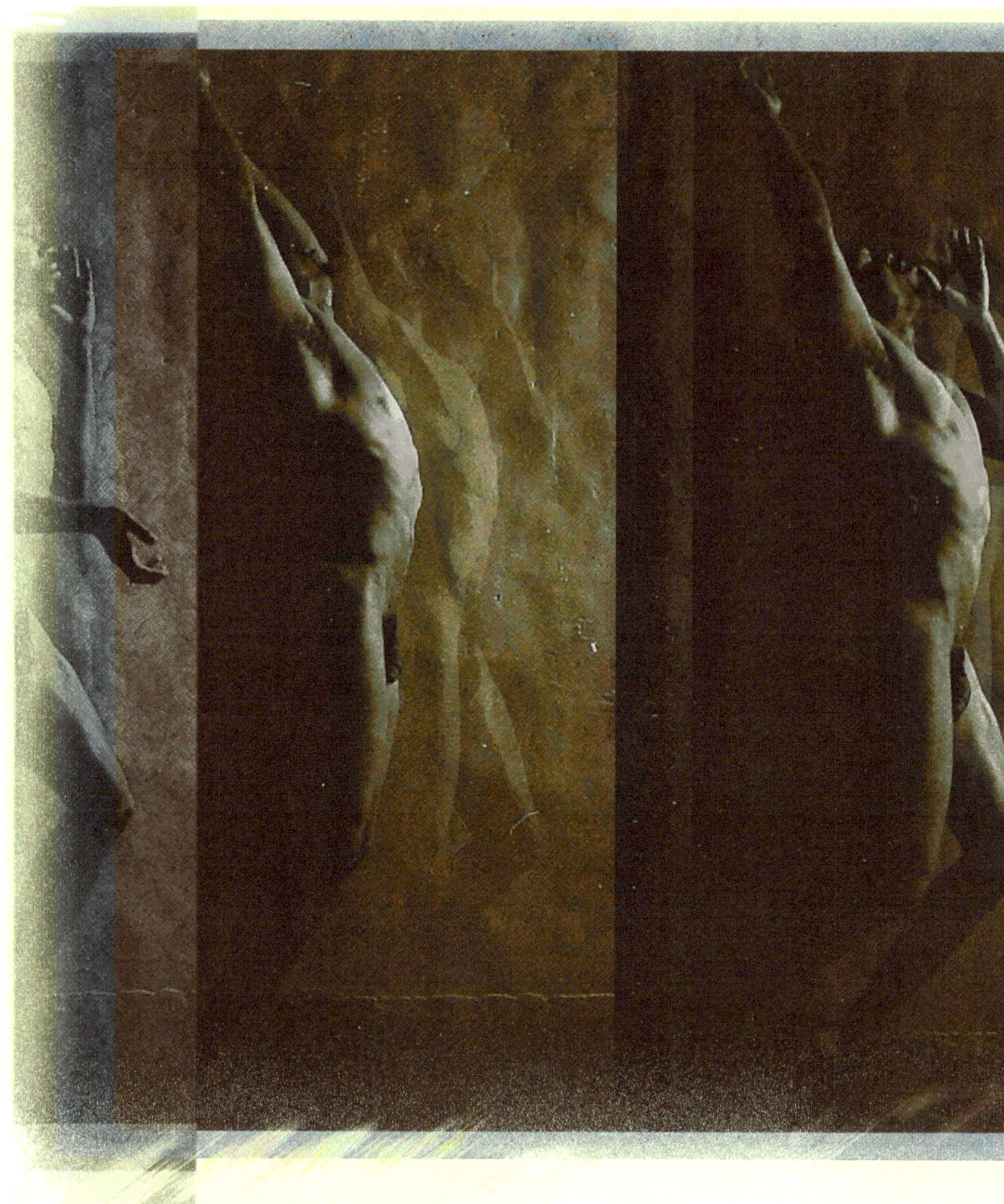

A Secret Told
1994 | digitally enhanced textured photograph
O.P.S. - 32" x 13"

There is more to me than this flesh. My chest emblazoned with weariness, eyes roll a few feet ahead waiting for the brain to catch on the slow sleekness of fermented body language.

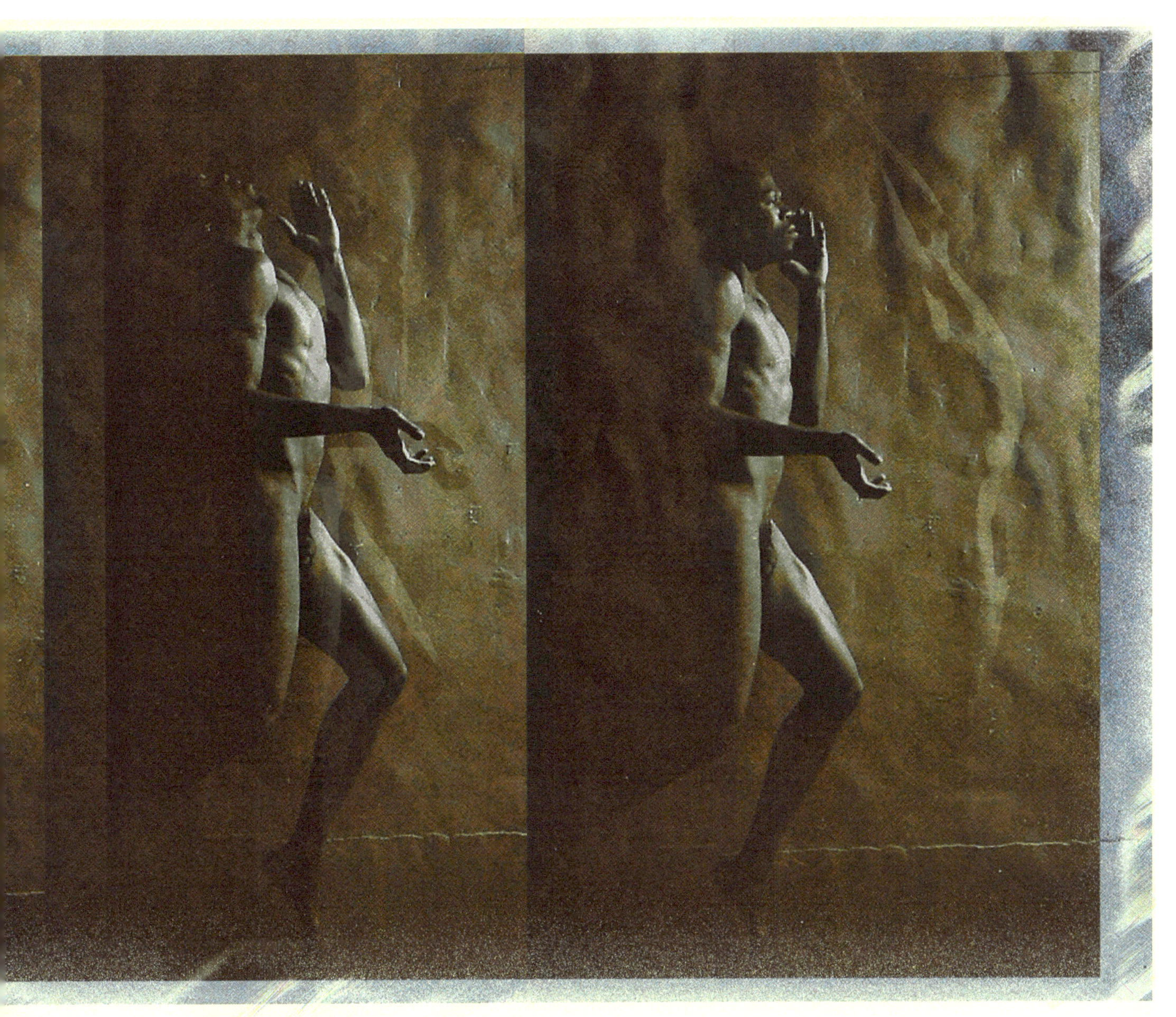

Pan Box
2000 | colorized B/W photo
O.P.S. - 24" x 30"

Dionysis cries with laughter, has spittle in the corners of this mouth, the corners that his mother sent him to when he was bad. He wants to succeed at the bacchanal, grow vines to blend with, and hold up the woodwork.

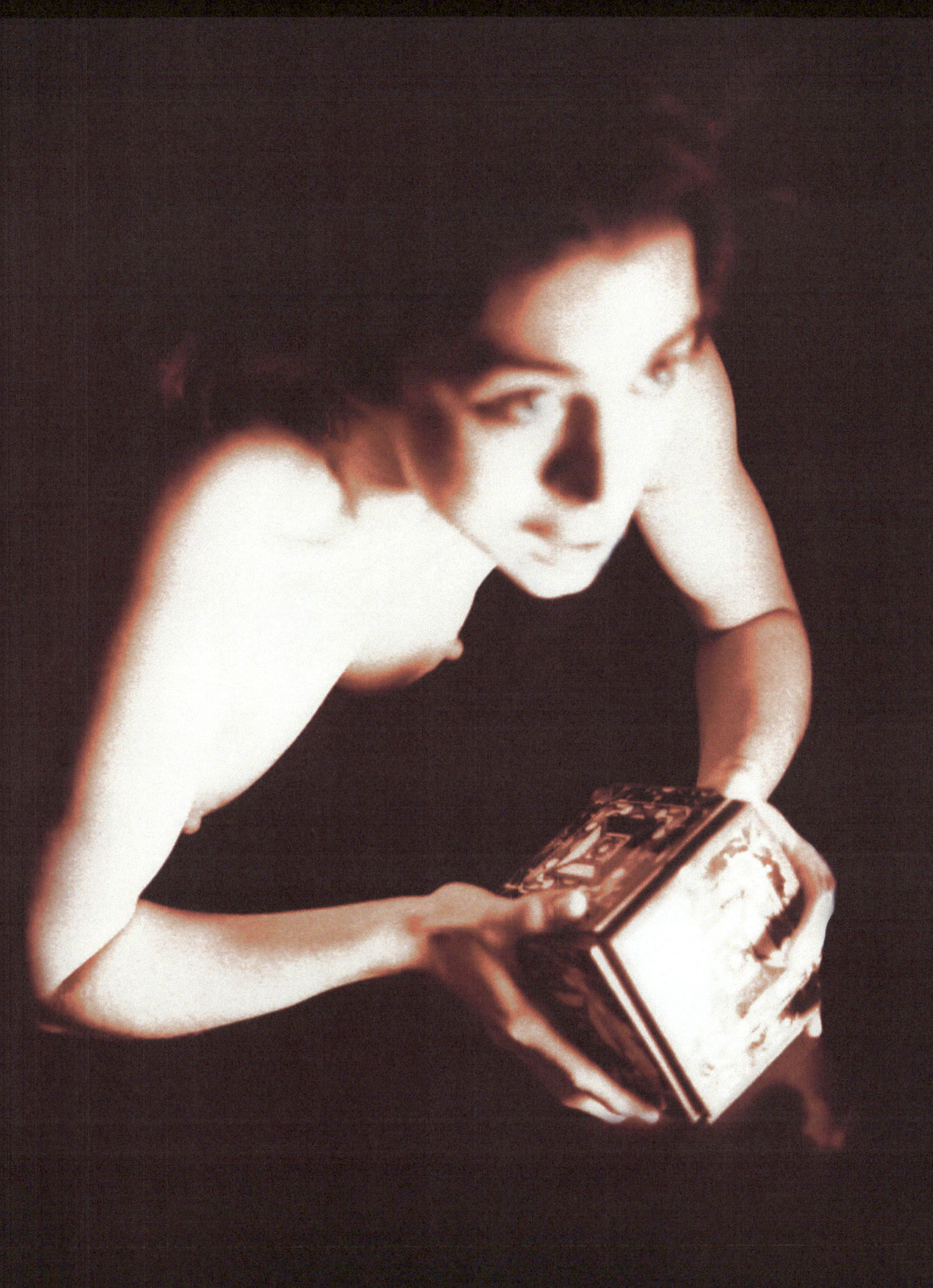

interloper

Mystery
1996 | B/W chemical photo colorized
O.P.S. - 17" x 11"

Twice now I've split my lip on your tongue.
Your all sharp kiss and bound passion.
How do I work this without being consumed by maybes?

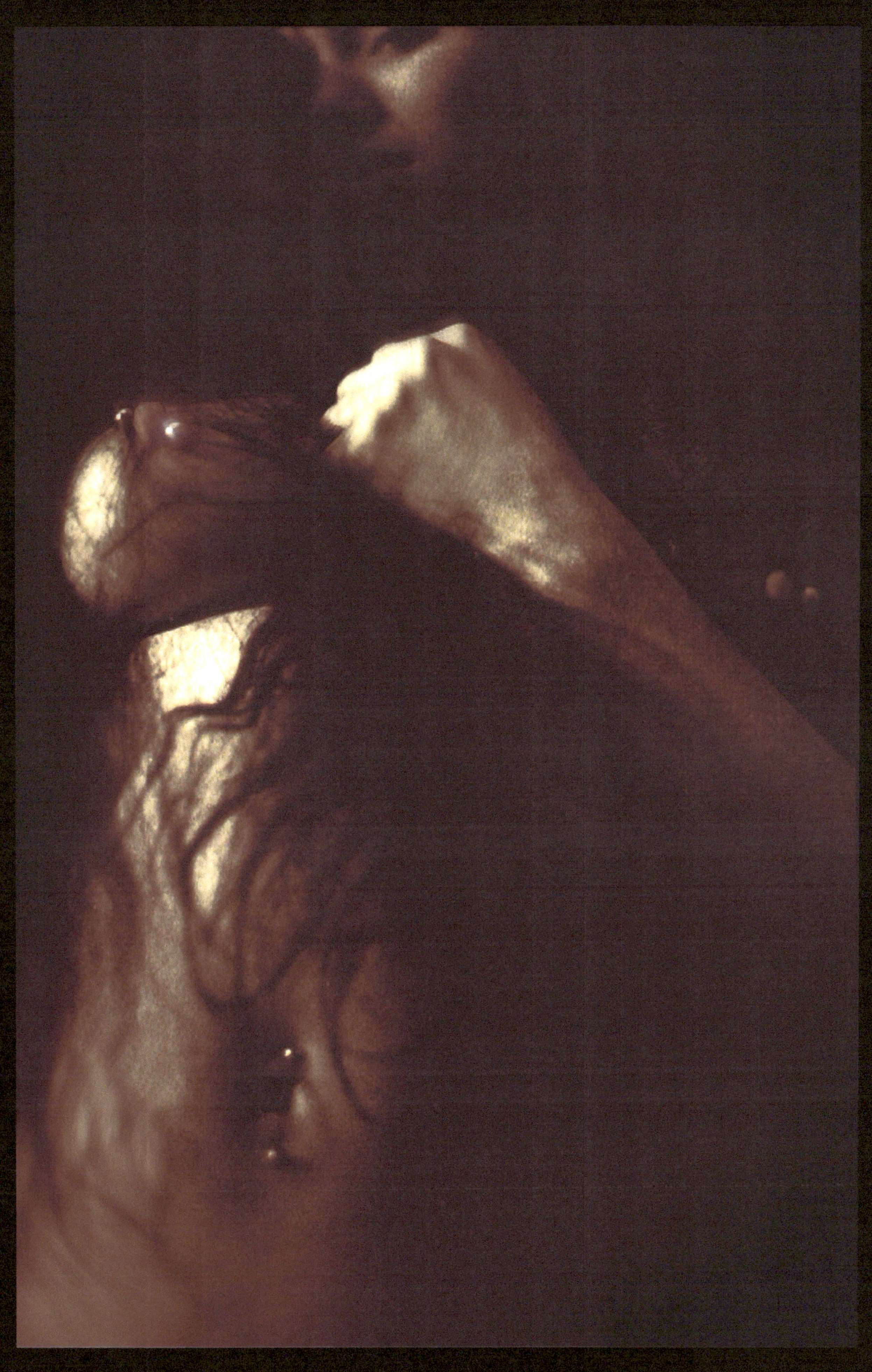

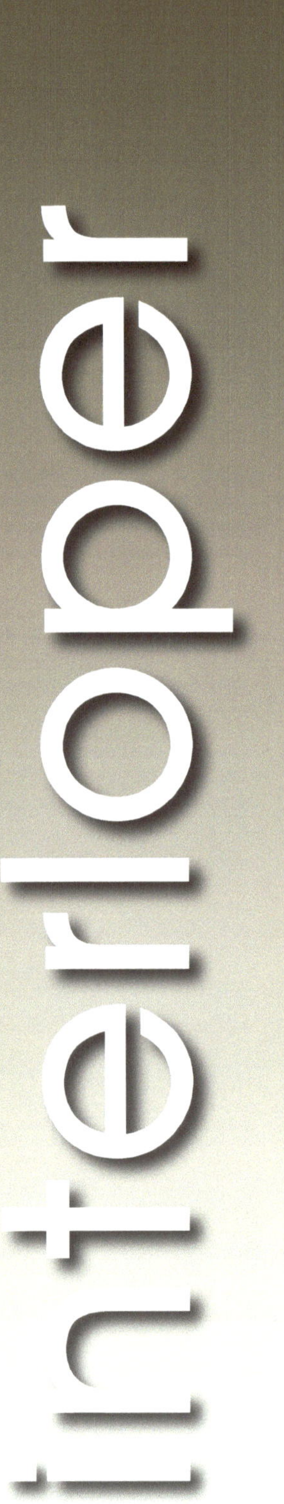

Working Woman
2004 | digitally enhanced, colorized photograph
O.P.S.- 24" x 44""

Cynical, critical of our toys
Once employed by others.
Our future
Lies singular.

Our void avoids
The building of our character
No one is home
The crowd bruises us,
Colorfully
And we seek visual stimulation.

Retina home
Retina of Rome
Oh, I see.
I can take it with me,
Whether I like it
Or
Not...

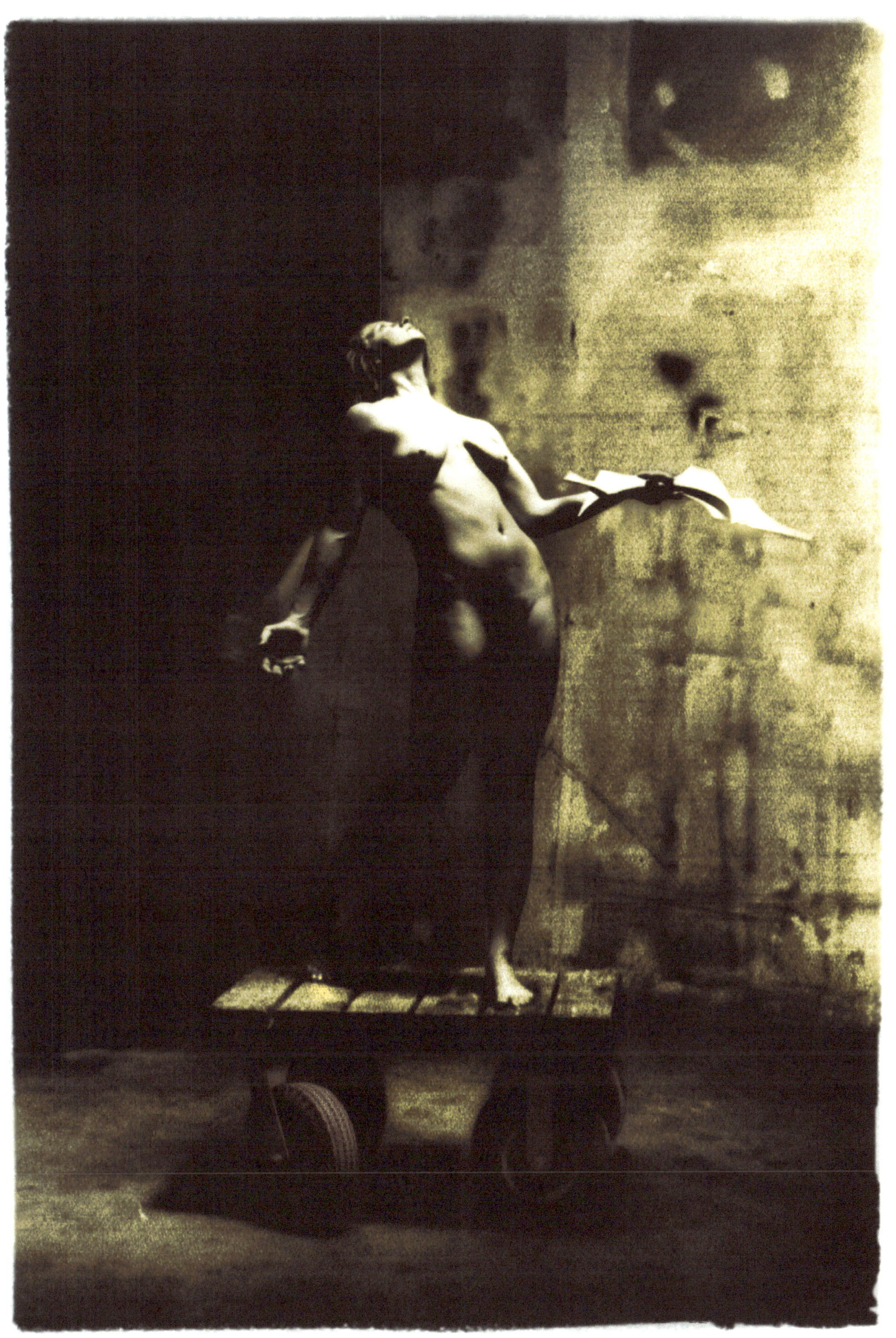

interloper

Velvet Vertebrae
1998 | mixed source photo-painting
O.P.S. - 13" x 20"

Spinning with without judgement,
To set free, to forget the sentence
That explains mouthed moist words.
Seedlings grow.
Sapling bends.
Sparking hands reach the sky, sighing,
Spirit unbreakable,
She's rising light, to her feet
For the sake of the dizziness of the fall

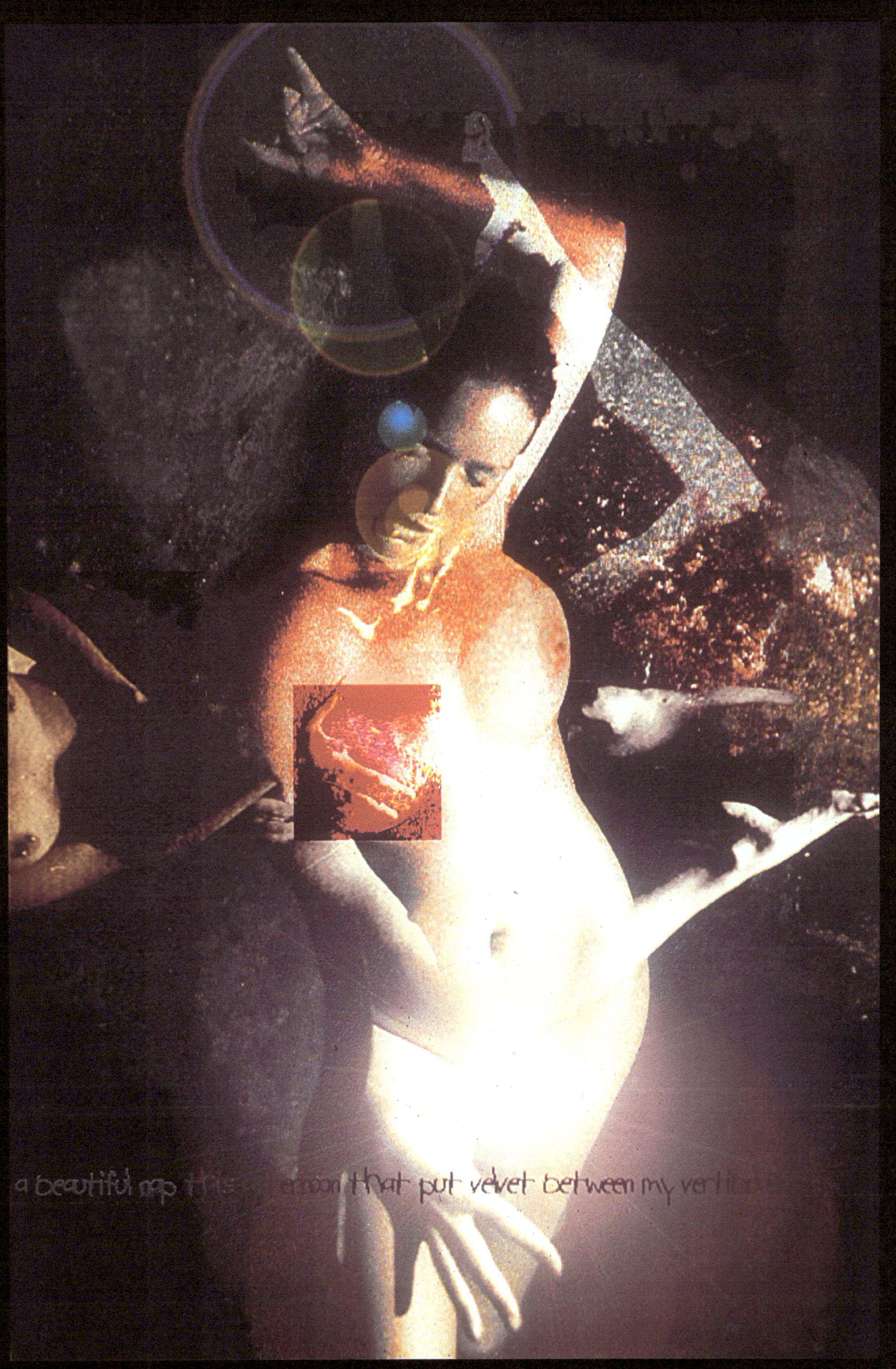
a beautiful nap
that put velvet between my

interloper

Clouds in the way
2000 | mixed source photo-painting.
O.P.S. - 24" x 36"

Extending arms
With growth boldly displayed
Changing patterns in a symphony
Of light and breeze
Becoming a kaleidoscope or canopy
In spirit in innate ability.

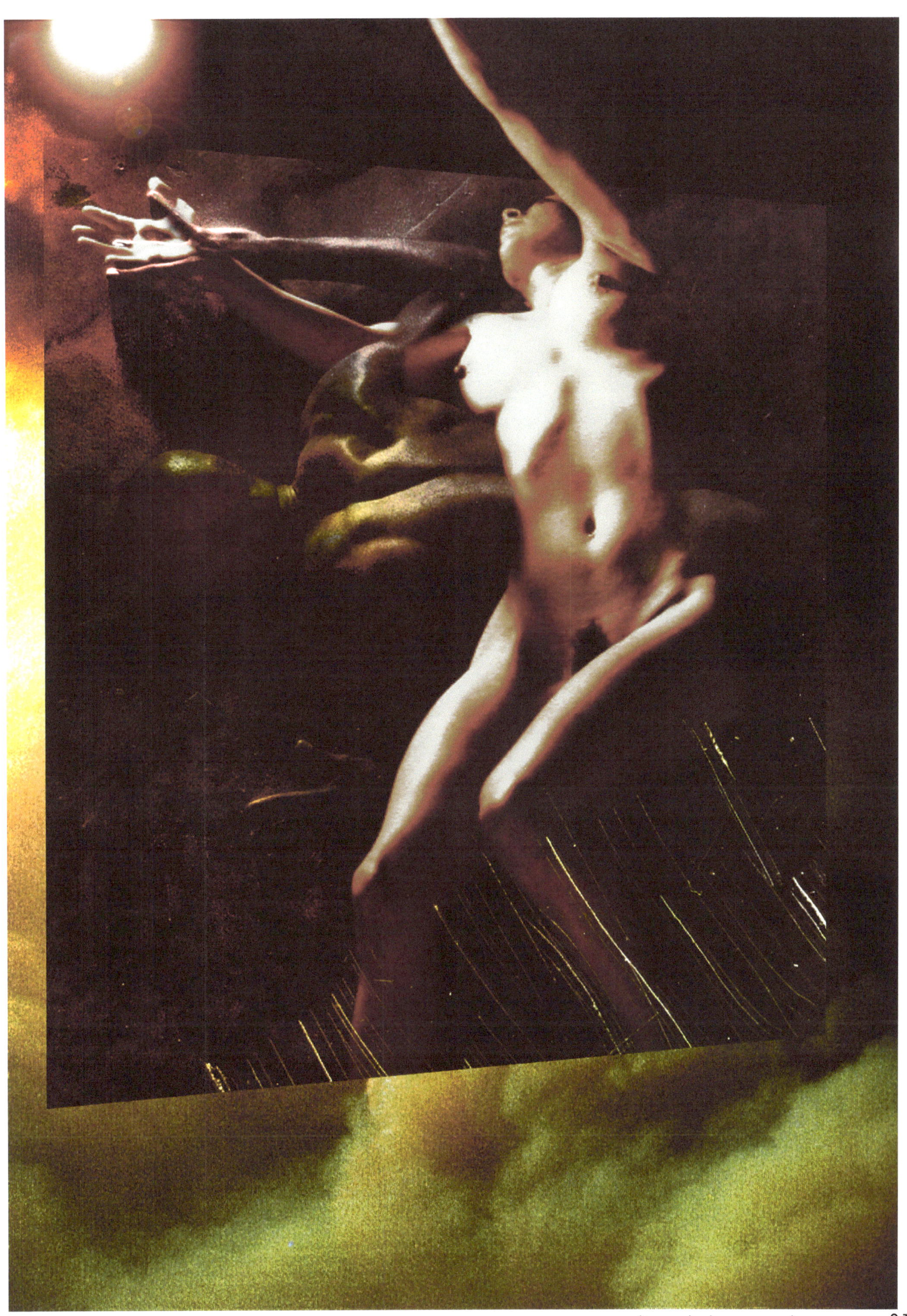

The brambles
2005 | digitally enhanced textured photograph
O.P.S. - 24" x 36"

Rending a new row...
To plant oh so very, oh so very many to grow at the touch of
Water that runs oh so very wild...

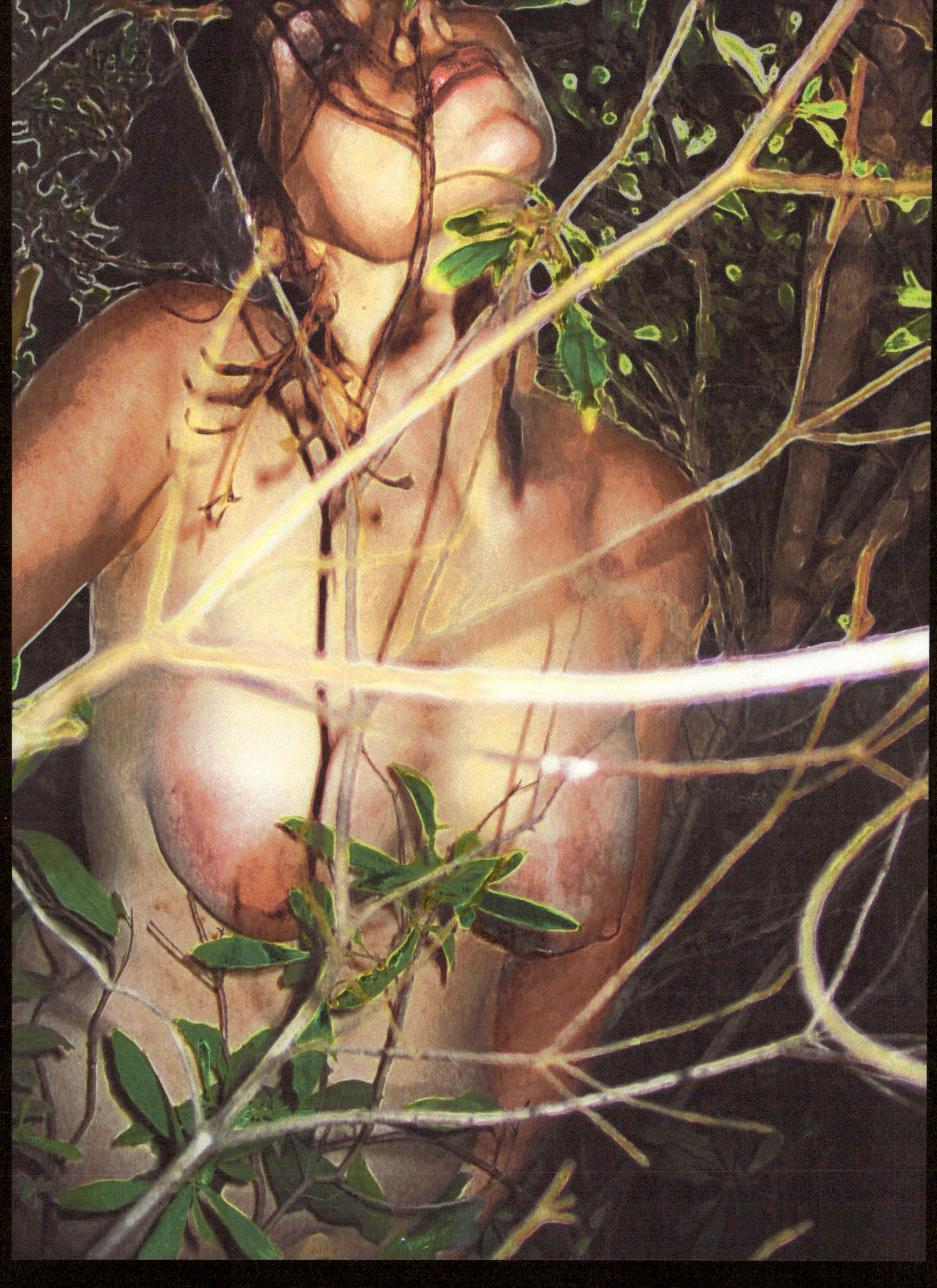

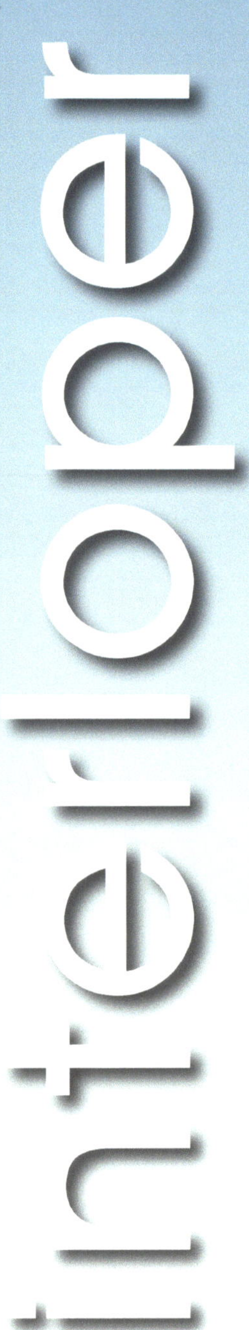

A fall to earth
2000 | mixed source photo-painting
O.P.S. - 24" x 42"

Passion grounds us.
Making gravity the world's best aphrodisiac.
Colors of cool, with
Blinding expulsion,
Of voice ringing,
Ears.
Testimony of will
"I will, I will."
This gravity of push
Sound ricochet,
Thought others run from,
Embraced in moments
Of lucid pre-dawn.
A new millennium.
Catching fire by the tail,
Electric spark of spirit
Ignite in youth, hope,
Glowing embers
Warming in waning years.

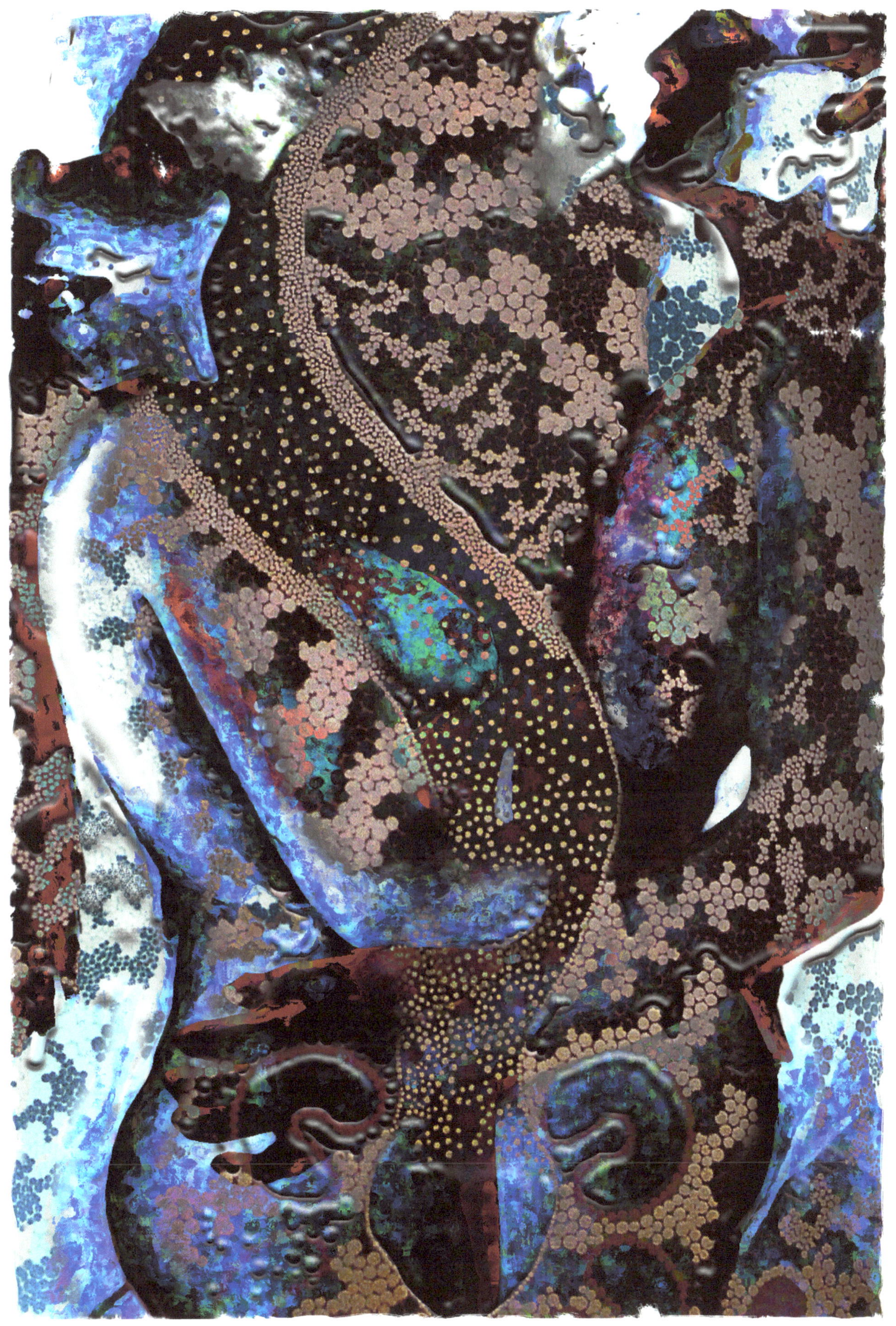

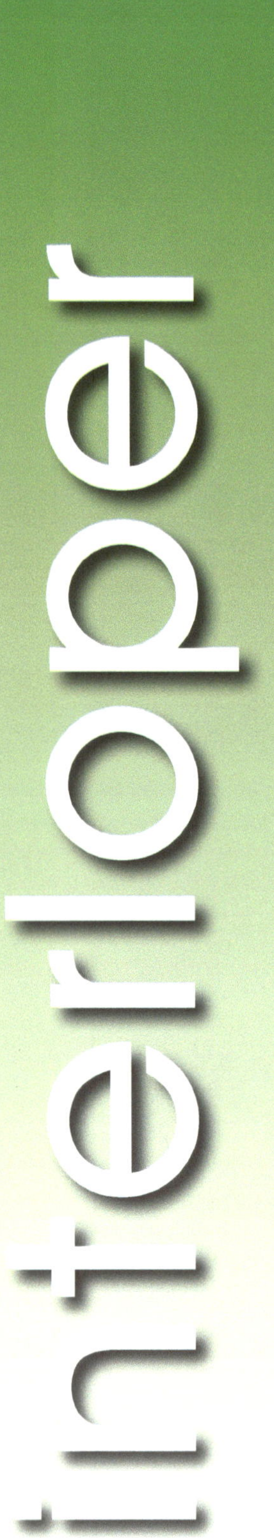

Angela in the wild
2005 | digitally enhanced textured photograph / organic distressing after printing
O.P.S. - 20" x 42"

A wild thing after a day in the civilized world.
I see it now, my inability to see
Both frightening and beautiful.
My groping, callused hands tend towards
Abandon and barbed wire.
Climbing this obstacle makes my life worthwhile
And my blood count lower

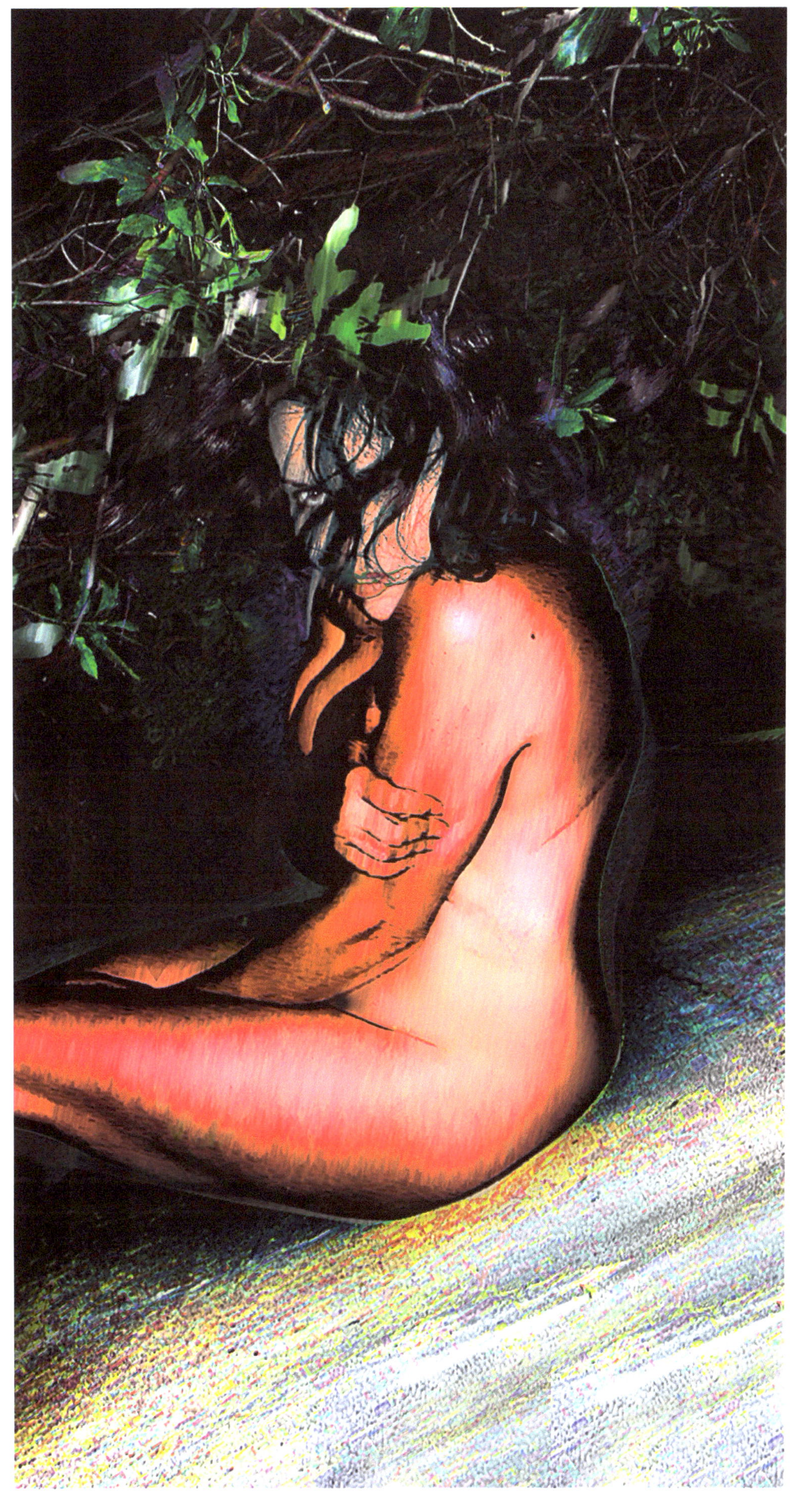

interloper

A lucky kiss
2000 | photo based composition
O.P.S. - 24" x 42"

The seduction of neon and alcohol. The music is the music contained in the wax sealed preserves of our heart. Not breaking the seal is everything here. Hear the muffled beat and whispered tune pitching you precariously close to dancing, here at the home for those skipping that beat, moving directly to the hidden meaning between the never ending lyric we retain like water.

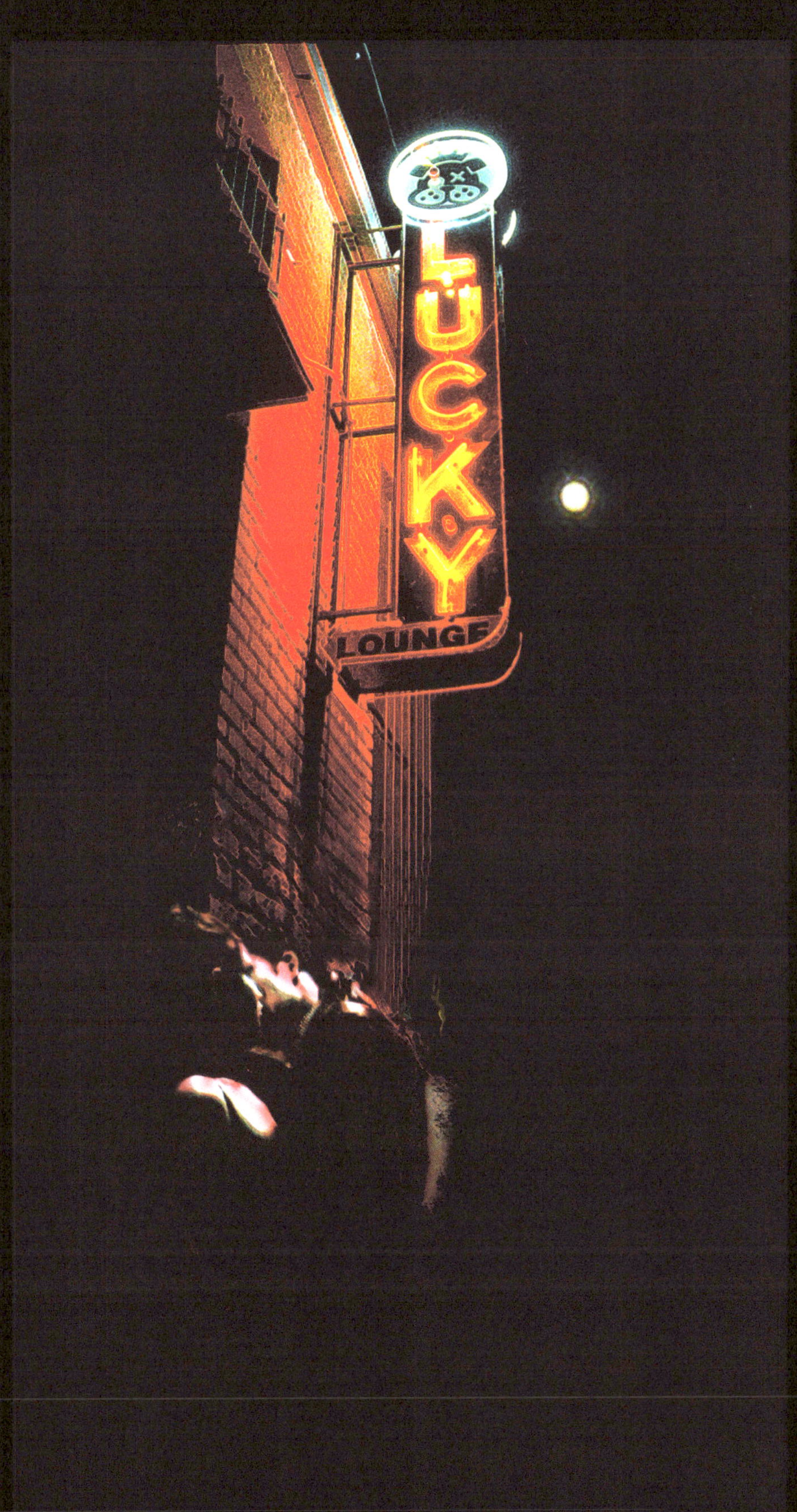
LUCKY
LOUNGE

interloper

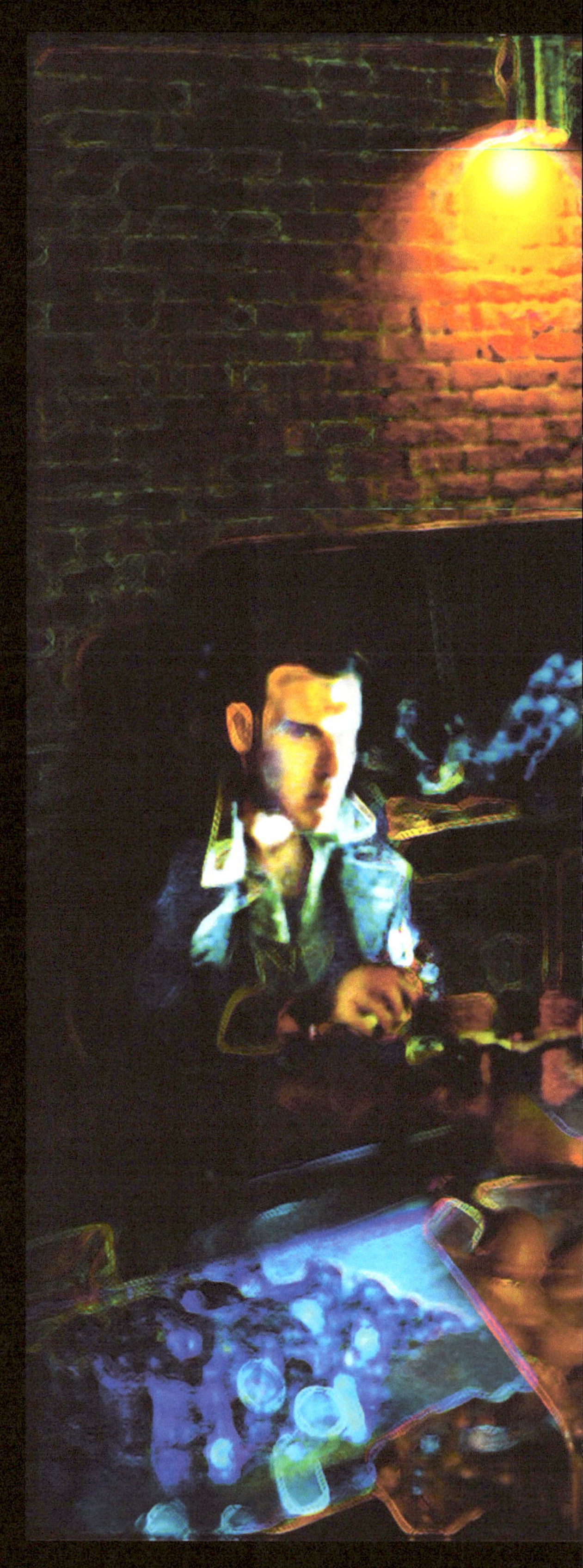

Couple 13
2001 | digitally enhanced textured photograph
O.P.S. - 36" x 24"

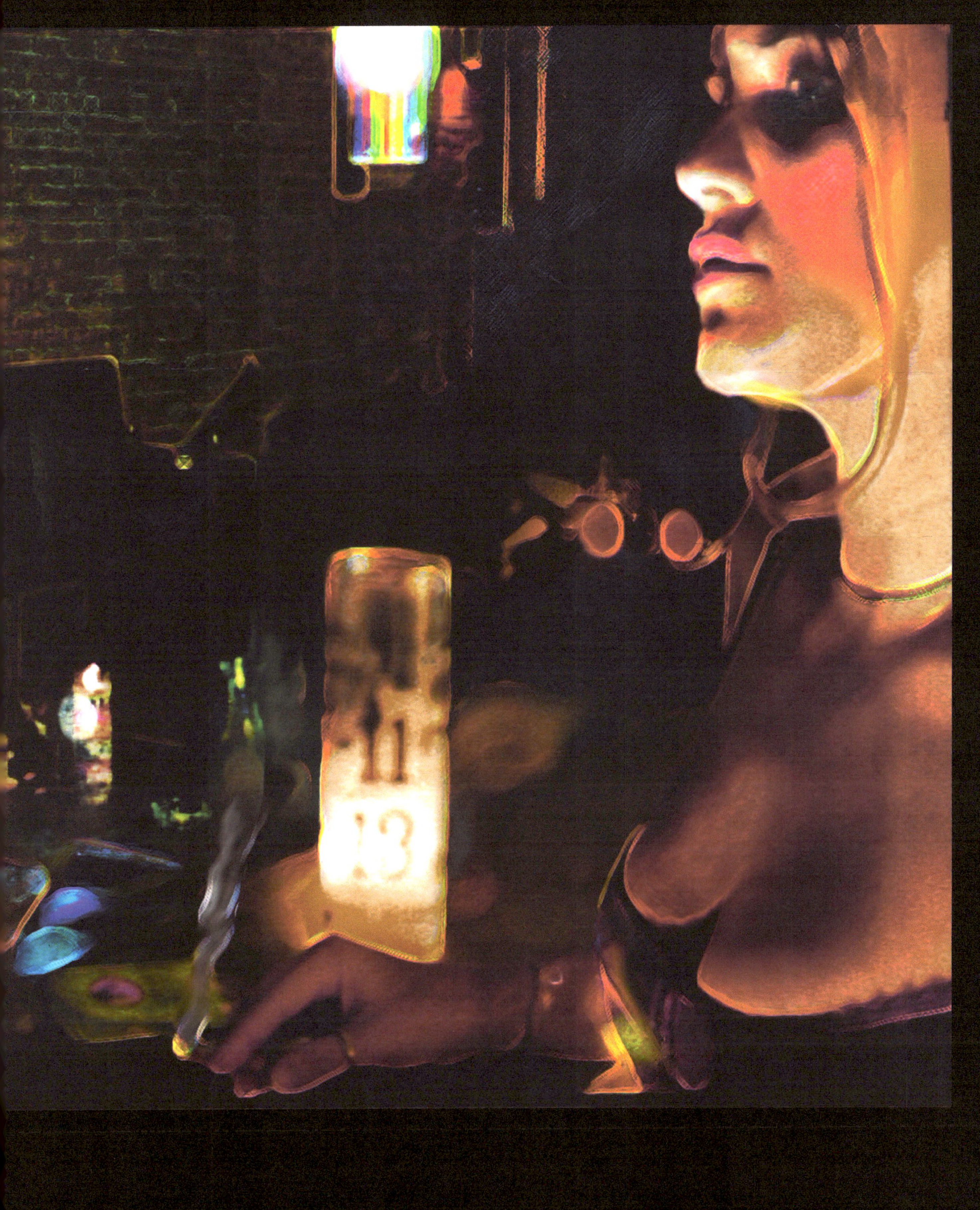

interloper

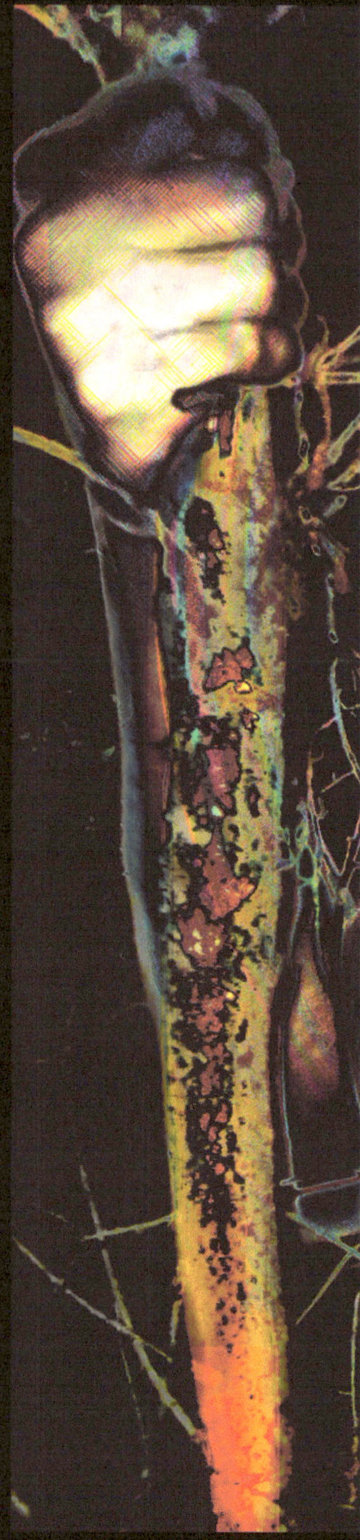

Night swim
2005 | mixed source photo-painting
O.P.S. - 42" x 28"

The promise of drama
The hope of provocation
Says that some things are unavoidable.
We are drawn to the need in now.
We avoid nothing in pursuit of real breath.
It keeps getting back to breathing. Always
The simplicity and comfort of oxygen.

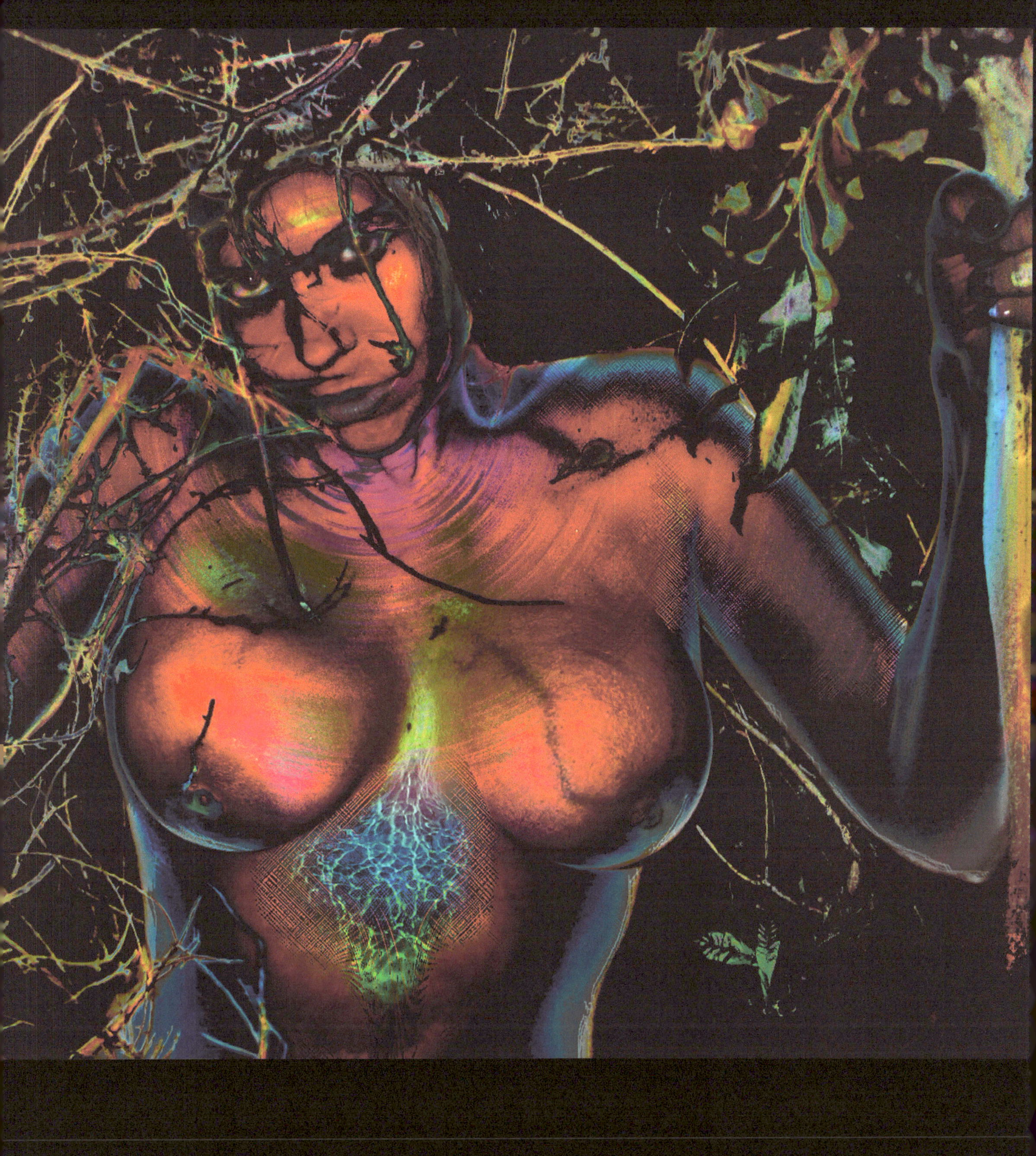

interloper

Sarah in Autumn
2003 | mixed source photo-painting
O.P.S. - 22" x 36"

The romance of discomfort
is what defines evolution

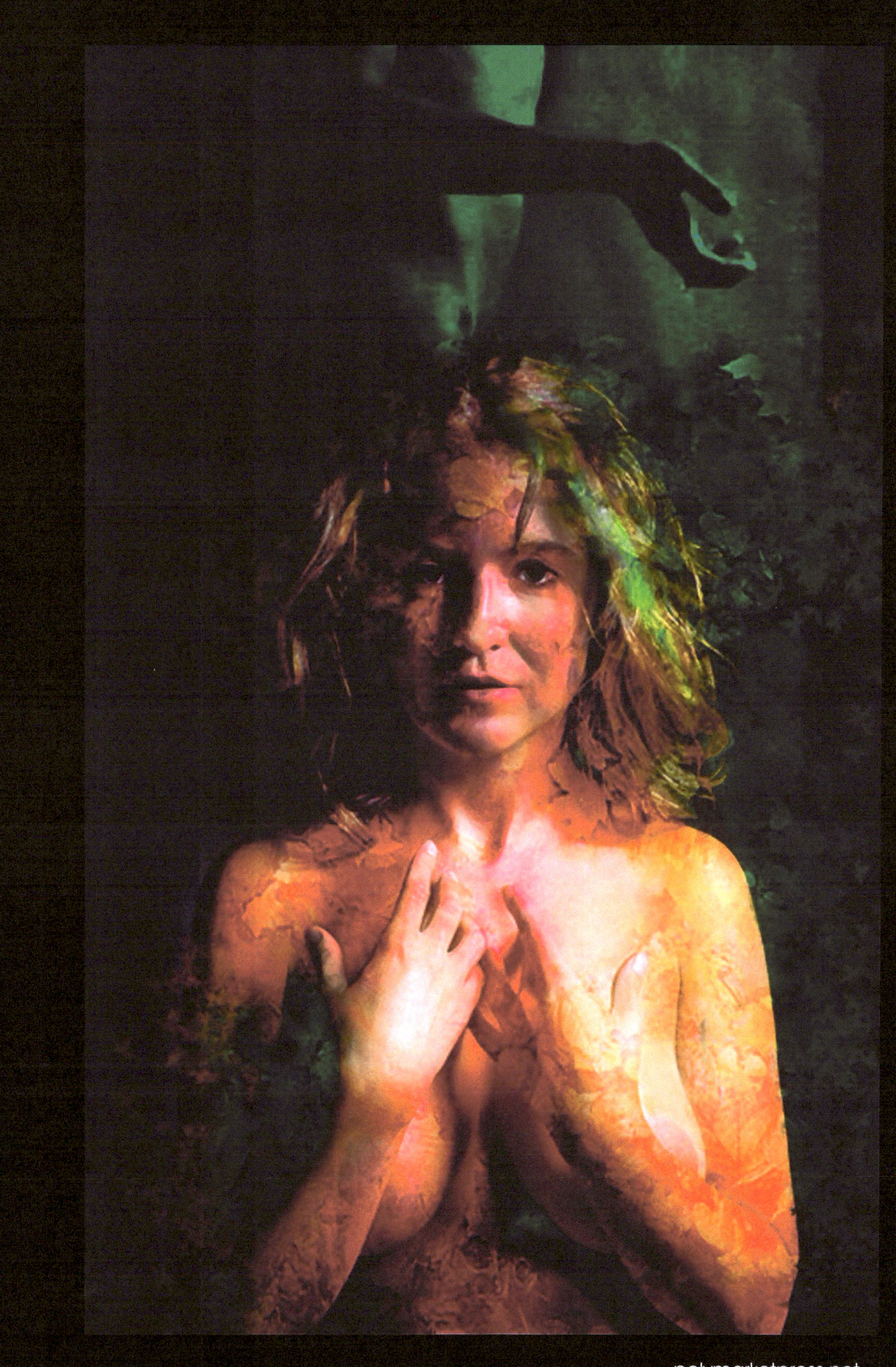

interloper

Pulling the heart down
2001 | mixed source photo-painting
O.P.S. - 48" x 34"

Medicated disorder
Concentrating on non thought
Odd snuff container
Found object fingernail resin
Poor on the text
Scratching the distress
Always the elements of a hammer

(art-work created & poem written in response to the attacks on the World Trade Center on 9/11/01)

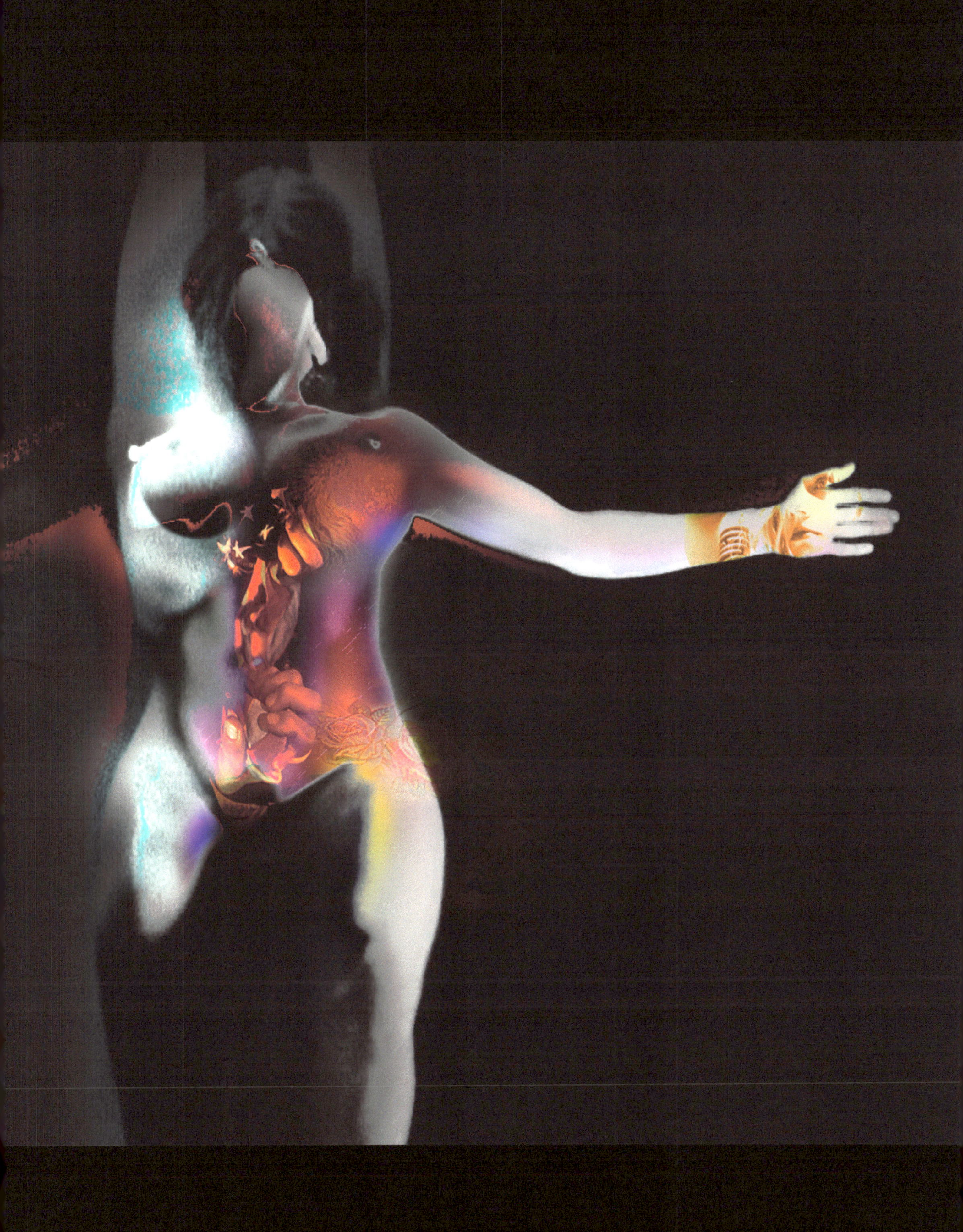

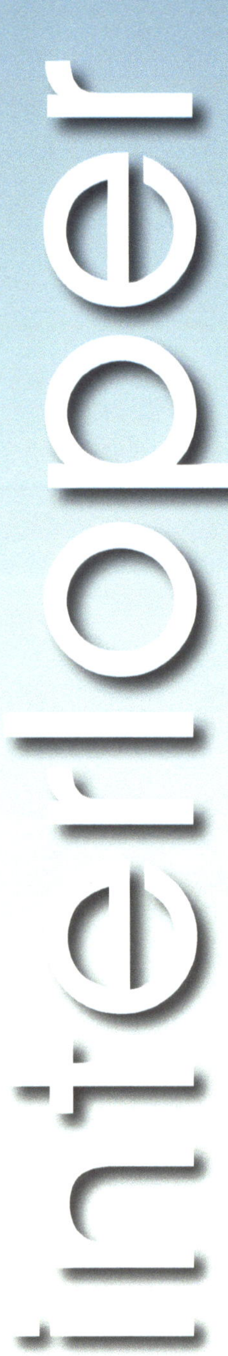

I of thee

2004 | mixed source photo-painting w/after print distressing.
O.P.S. - 32" x 52"

Hope me home rattle shack palsy, dance
shuffle repose.
Transposing faith into us like slow grooving
washing machines.
Purge the days stains with dangerous clapping hands.
A rhythm one to another.... one to another.

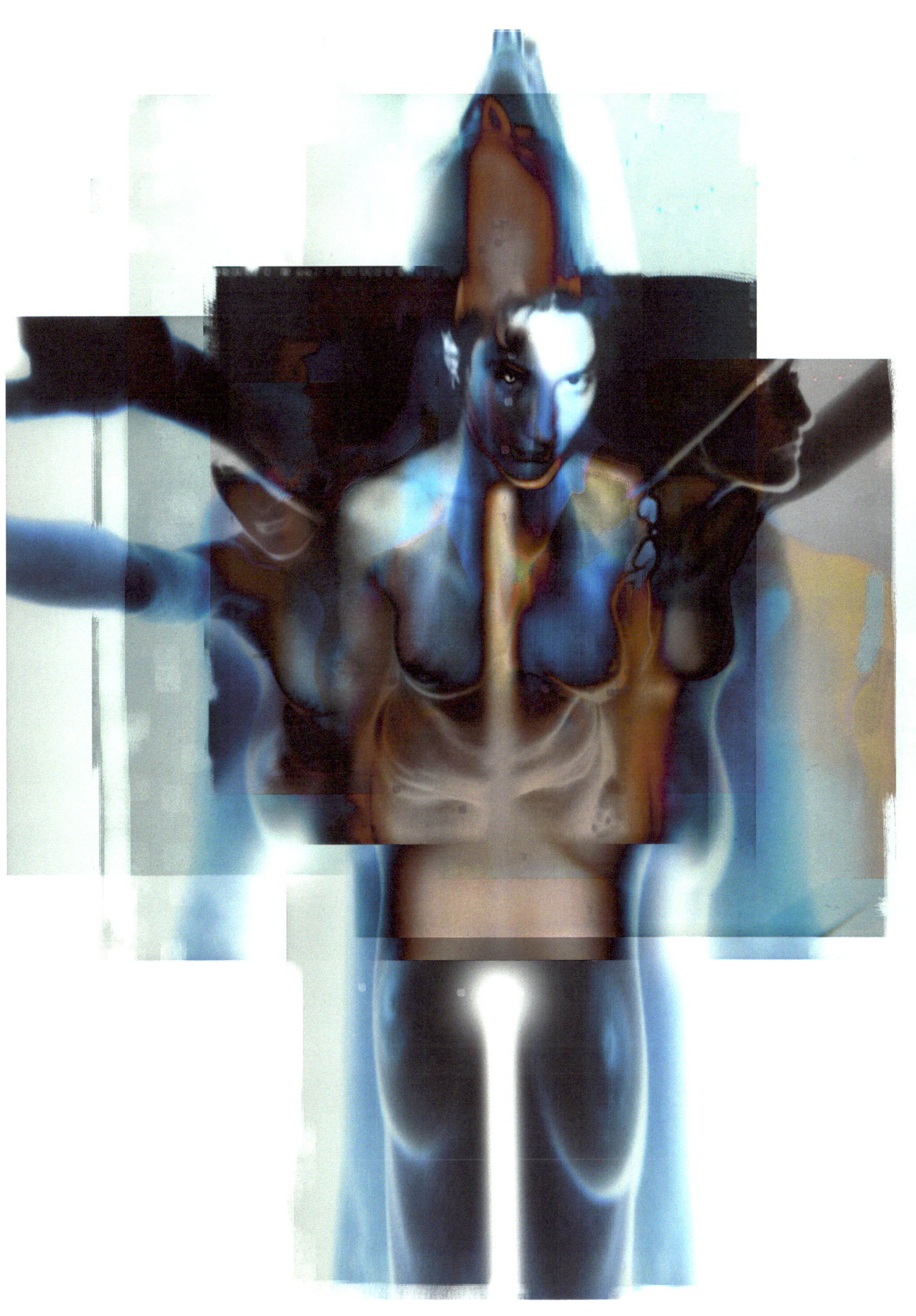

interloper

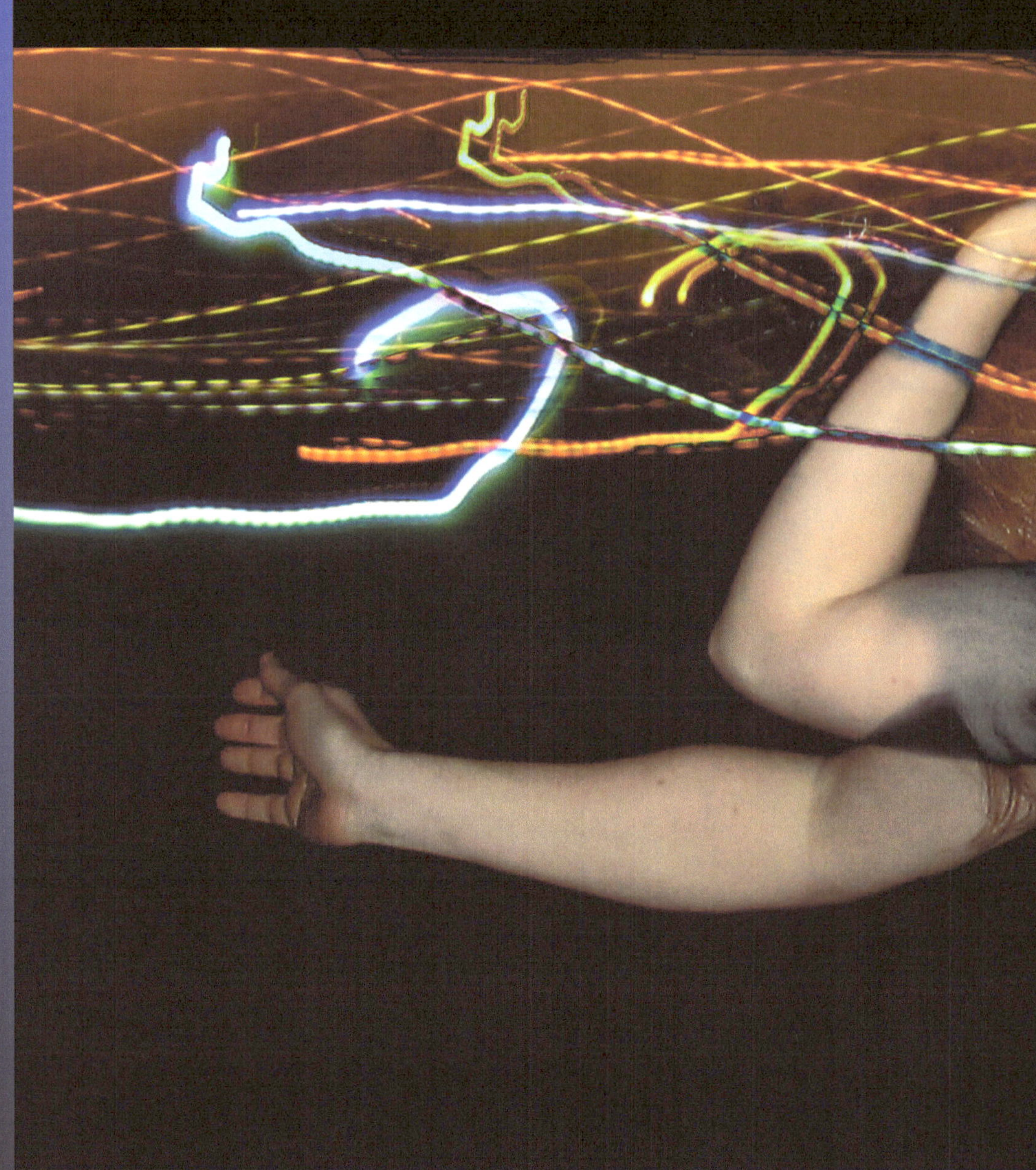

Night
2006 | digitally enhanced textured photograph
O.P.S. - 36" x 20"

All of you want me to no
When I want to yes
Confess to the stars
Your love for me to change
Your glow, your distance
From the sun

ricardo acevedo

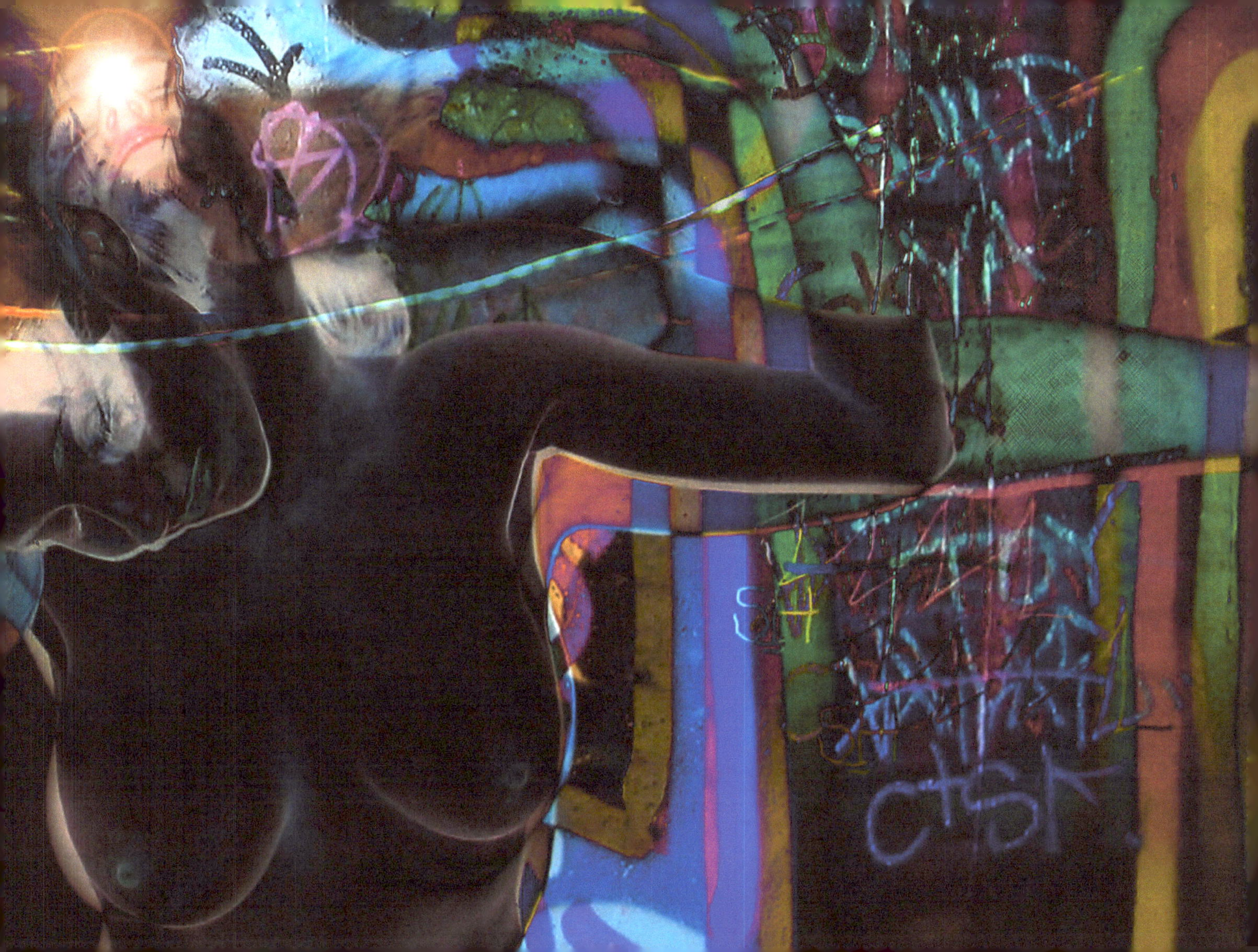

interloper

Fourth
2000 | mixed source photo-painting
O.P.S. - 14" x 42"

My mother screaming at the top of her lungs
About the rhythm of hips.
Senseless sister gropings in the darkness
Of abandon, defenseless

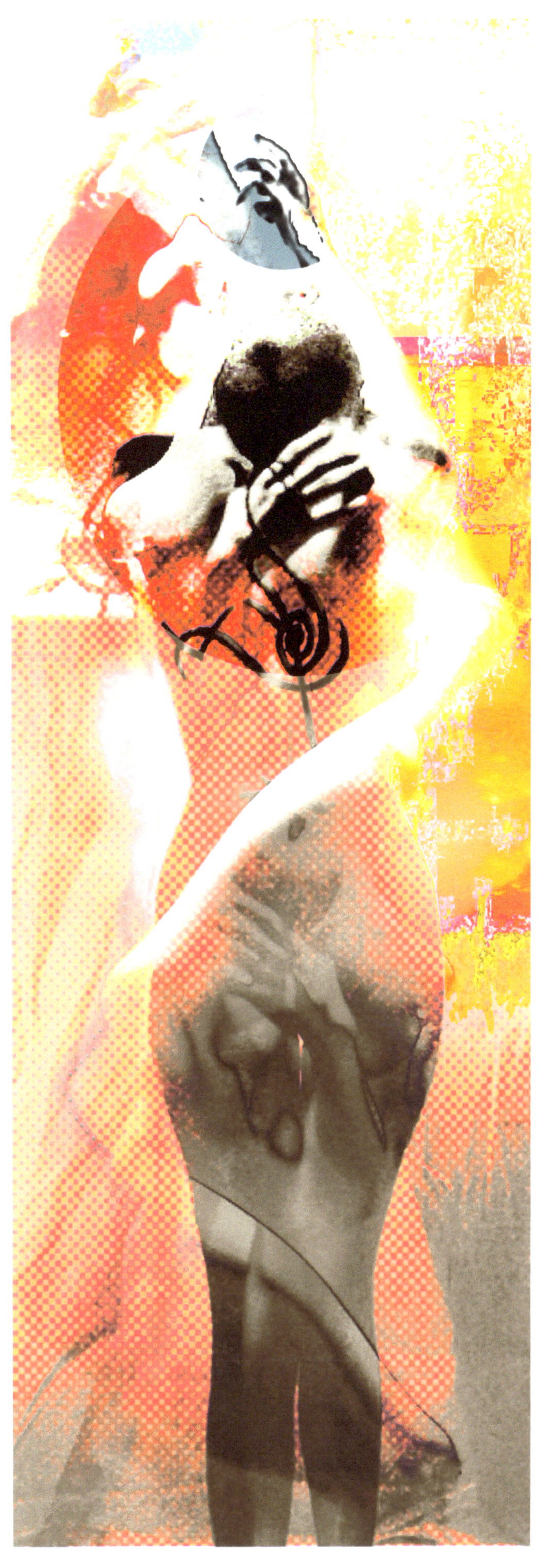

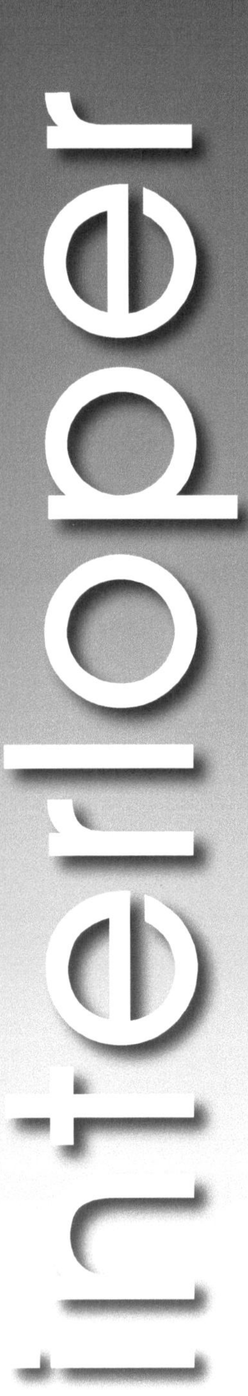

Through her
2004 | Mixed source photo-painting
O.P.S. - 20" x 42"

Terra firma mama drama
Open to the funk of karma

Tired of simulated hard-ons

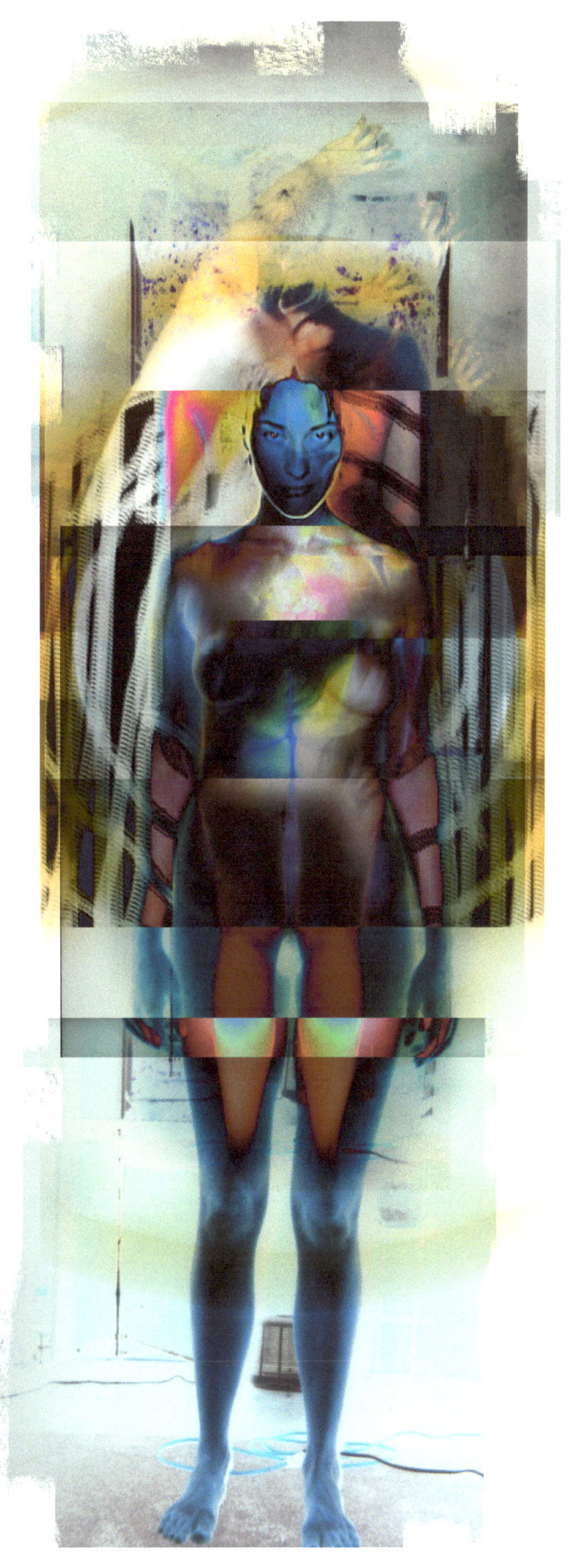

interloper

Lexi Smoke
2008 | mixed source photo-painting
O.P.S. - 28" x 48"

Picasso drew his tyrant
In a tornado.
She spins,
You blink and freeze the mouth
The destructive cleansing
Forced angle, harsh line
Away from your perception
Of nature
View point, pointed
But direct
And quick of her rapier
Makes you flinch.

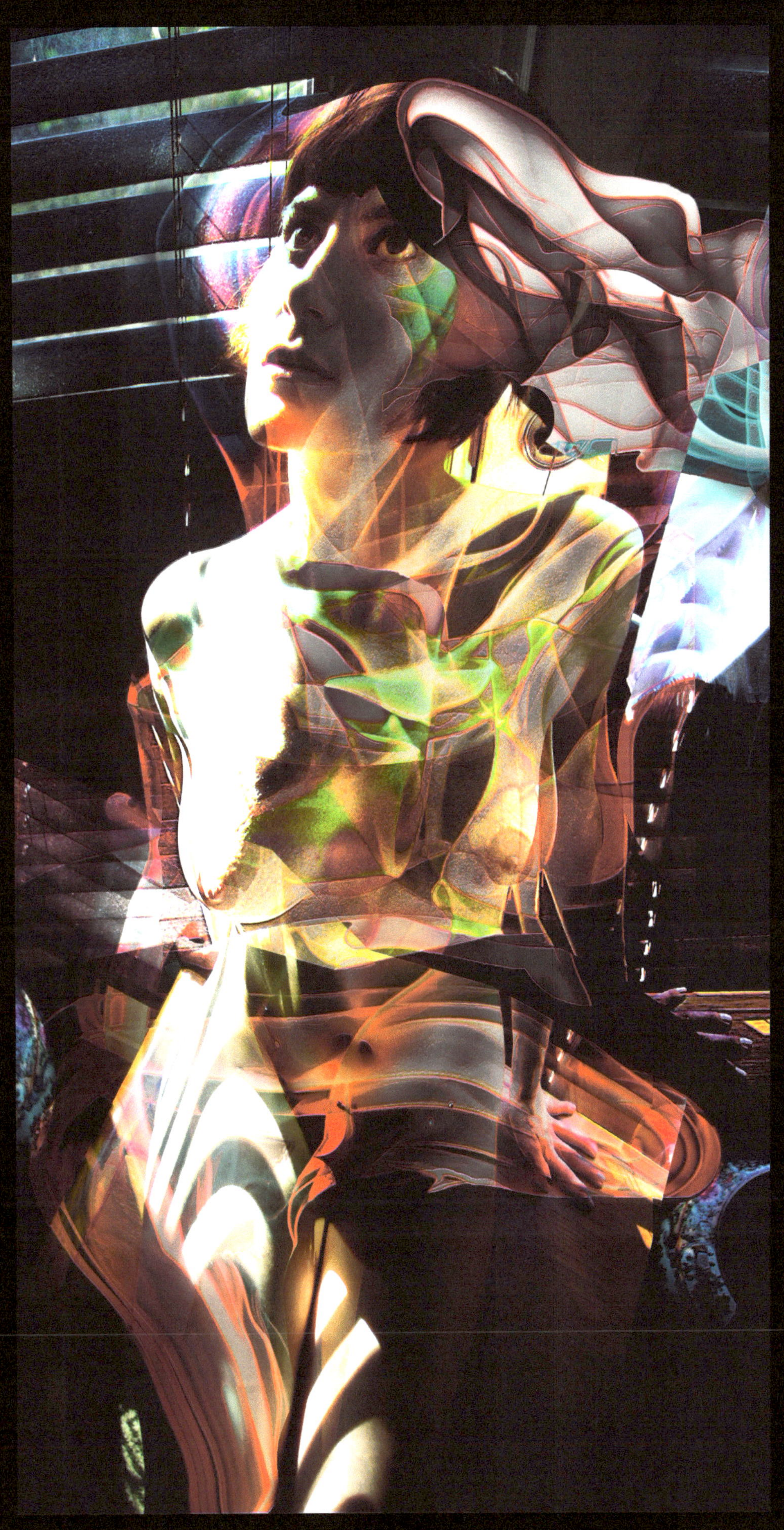

interloper

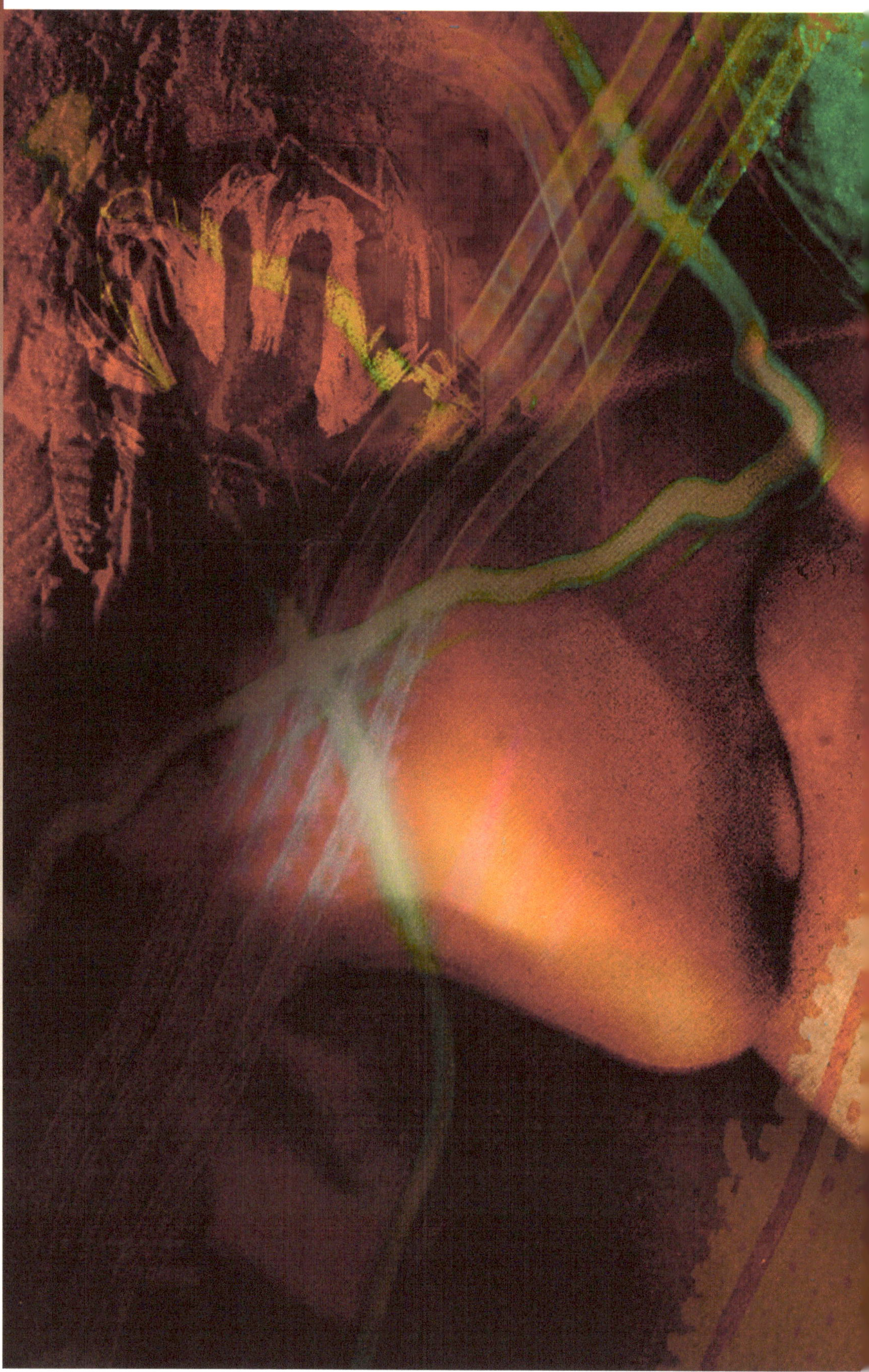

No Language
2004 | mixed source photo-painting
O.P.S. - 40" x 24"

ricardo acevedo

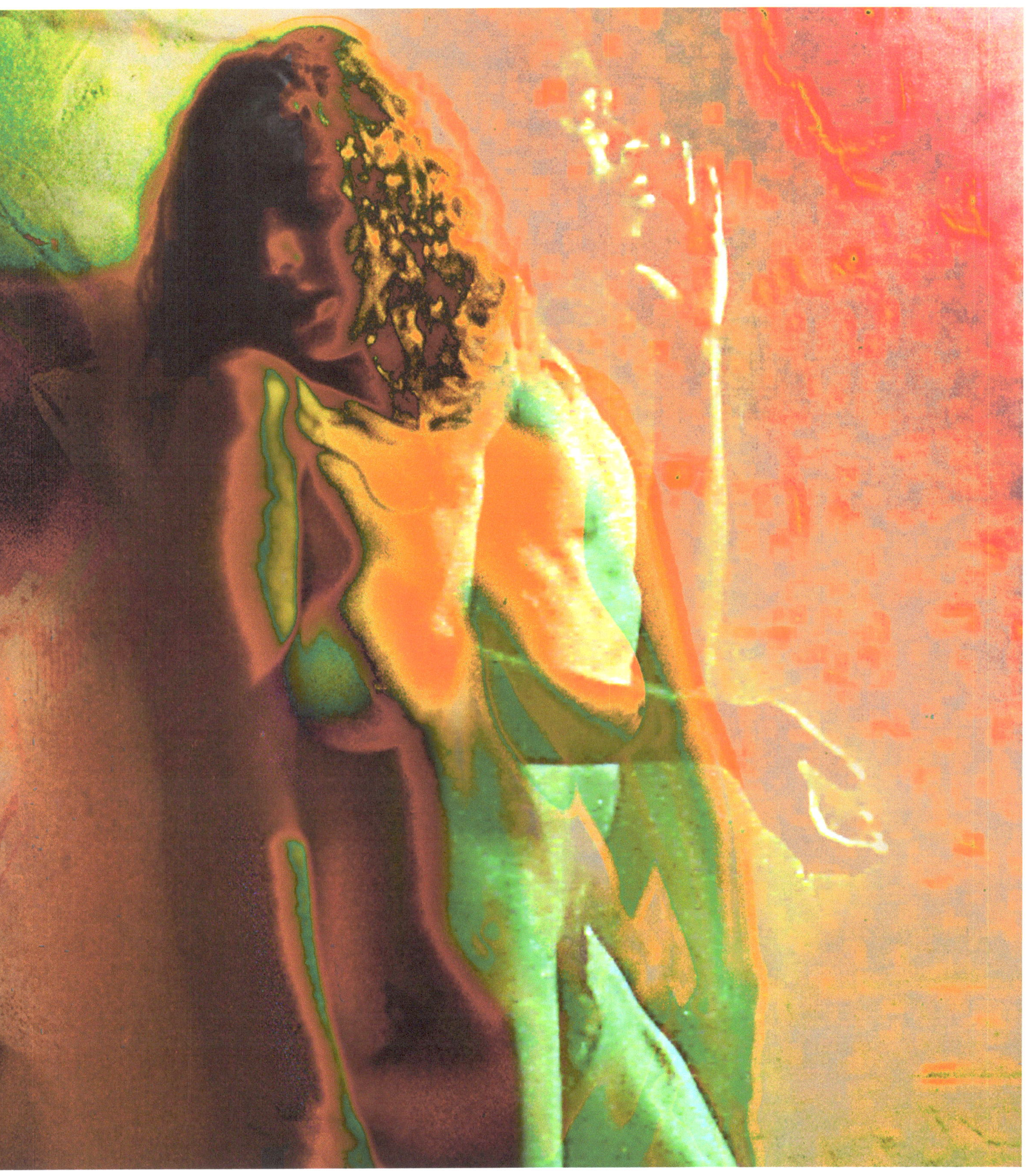

interloper

Traffic
2006 | digitally enhanced textured photograph
O.P.S. - 16" x 36"

Neon light gives them perspective out the window
It's a headlight bath
These things pull you and if you're lucky you get the warning
Of history sweet candy
and empty calories that ruin your smile.

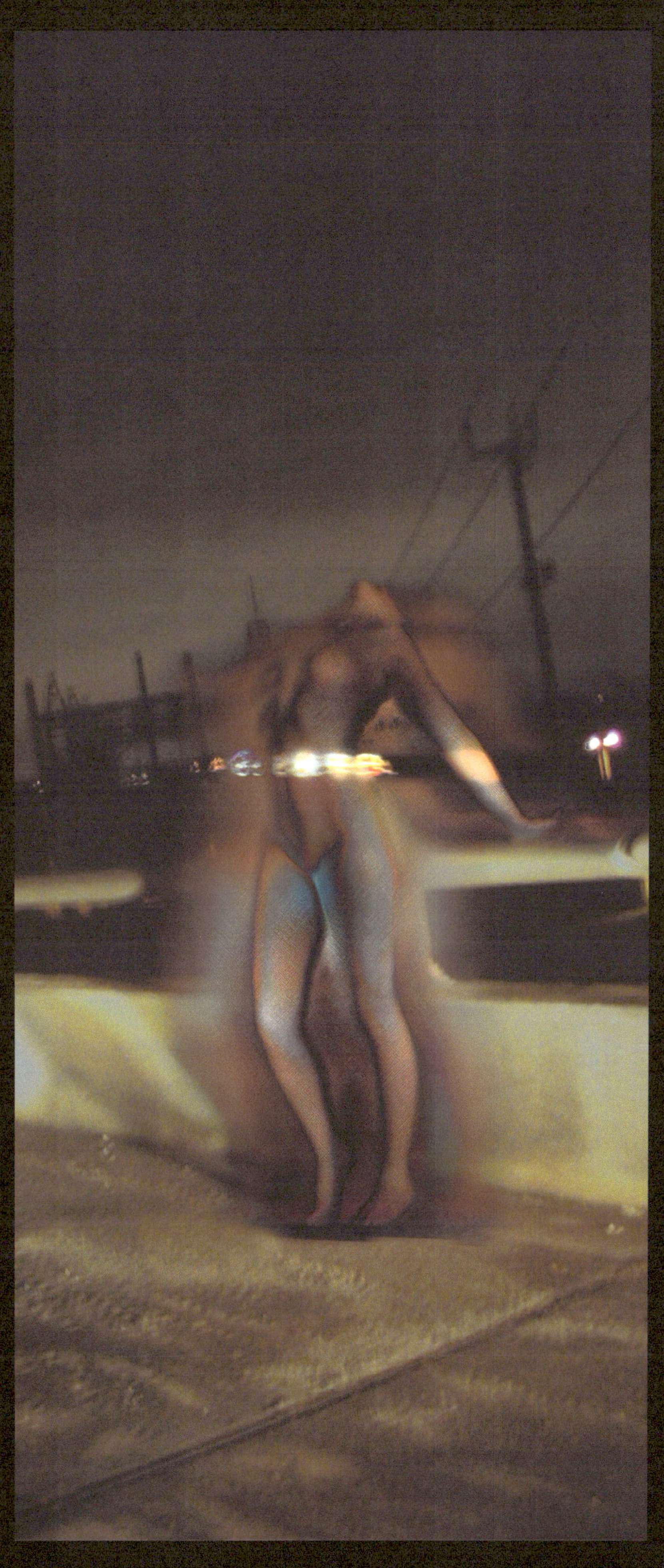

interloper

Alexis 1

2008 | digitally enhanced textured photograph.

O.P.S. - 24" x 42"

Venus as a hallucination walking on water

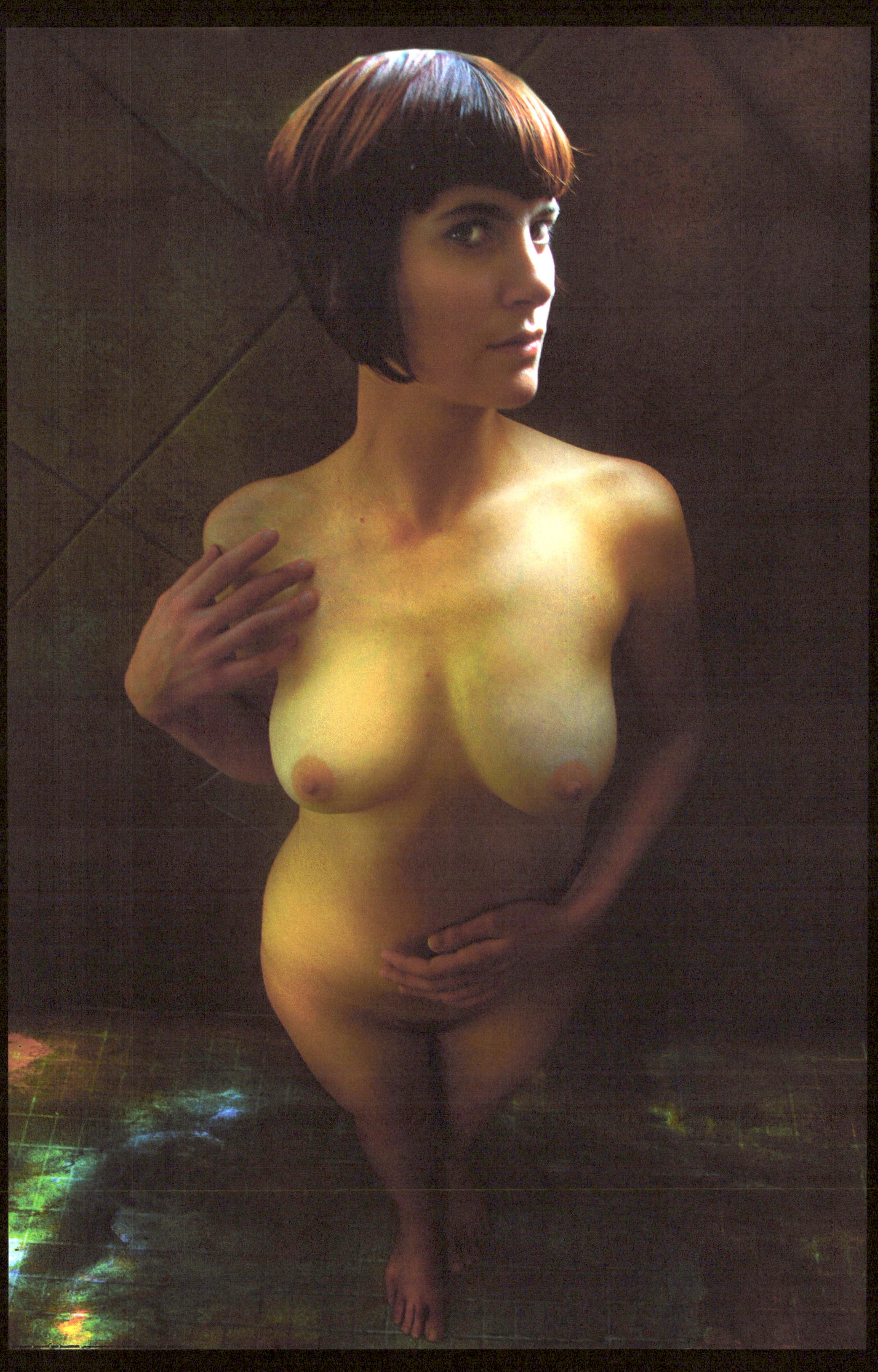

interloper

Buddha
2005 | digitally enhanced textured photograph
O.P.S. - 24" x 36"

Show me the colors that you turn
The burls your twisted ways won't hide
The scars your efforts have endowed and
Till the flowering fruits you bear as gifts
For those who come to honor and partake
In this nurturing explosion you create

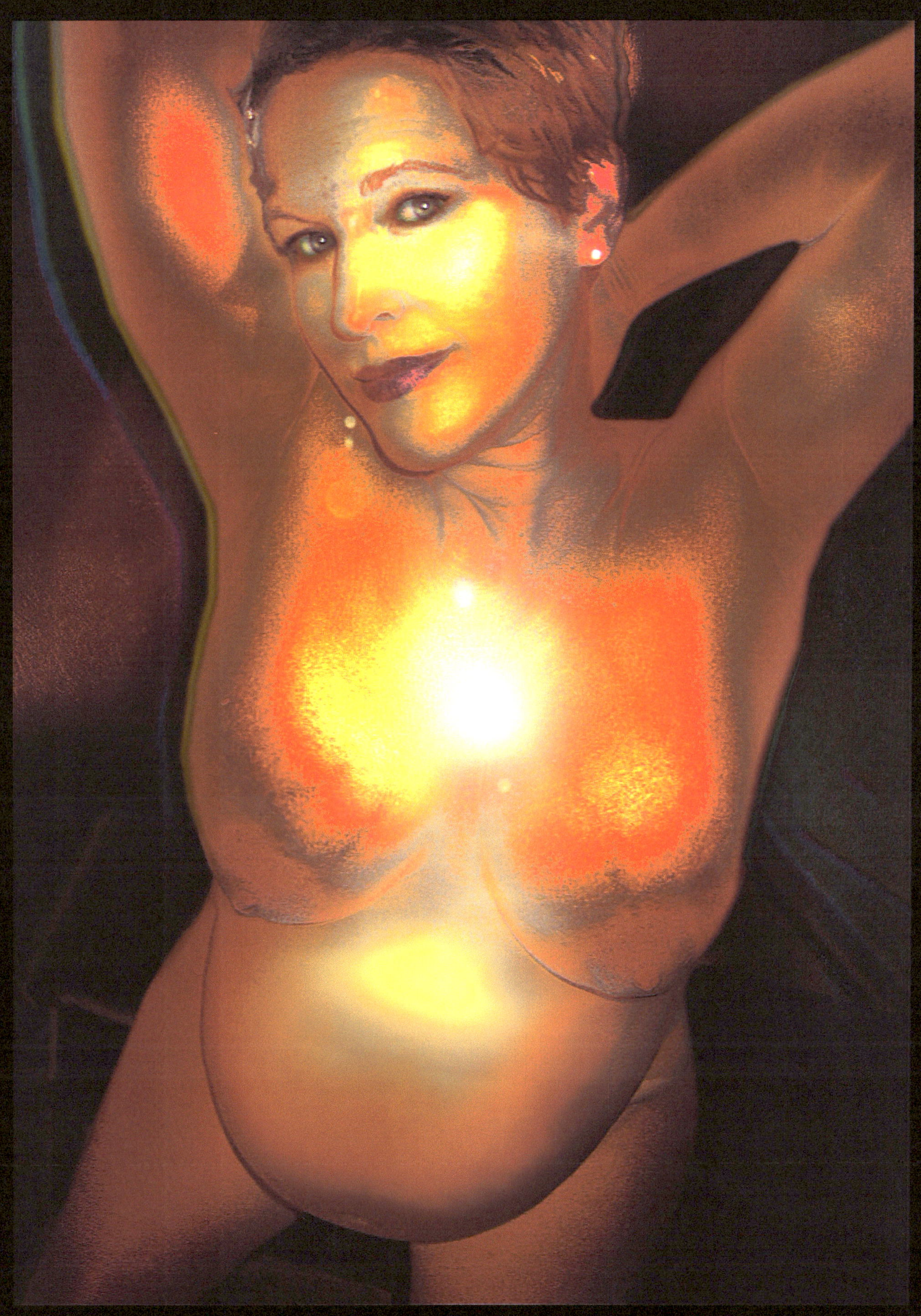

interloper

Push
2007 | digitally enhanced textured photograph.
O.P.S. - 24" x 30"

Within inches of my hand your beating heart could grind to silence so simply, as slow and careless as dawn bringing blue haze down, calling shadows up from earth and floors, from bedroom corners.

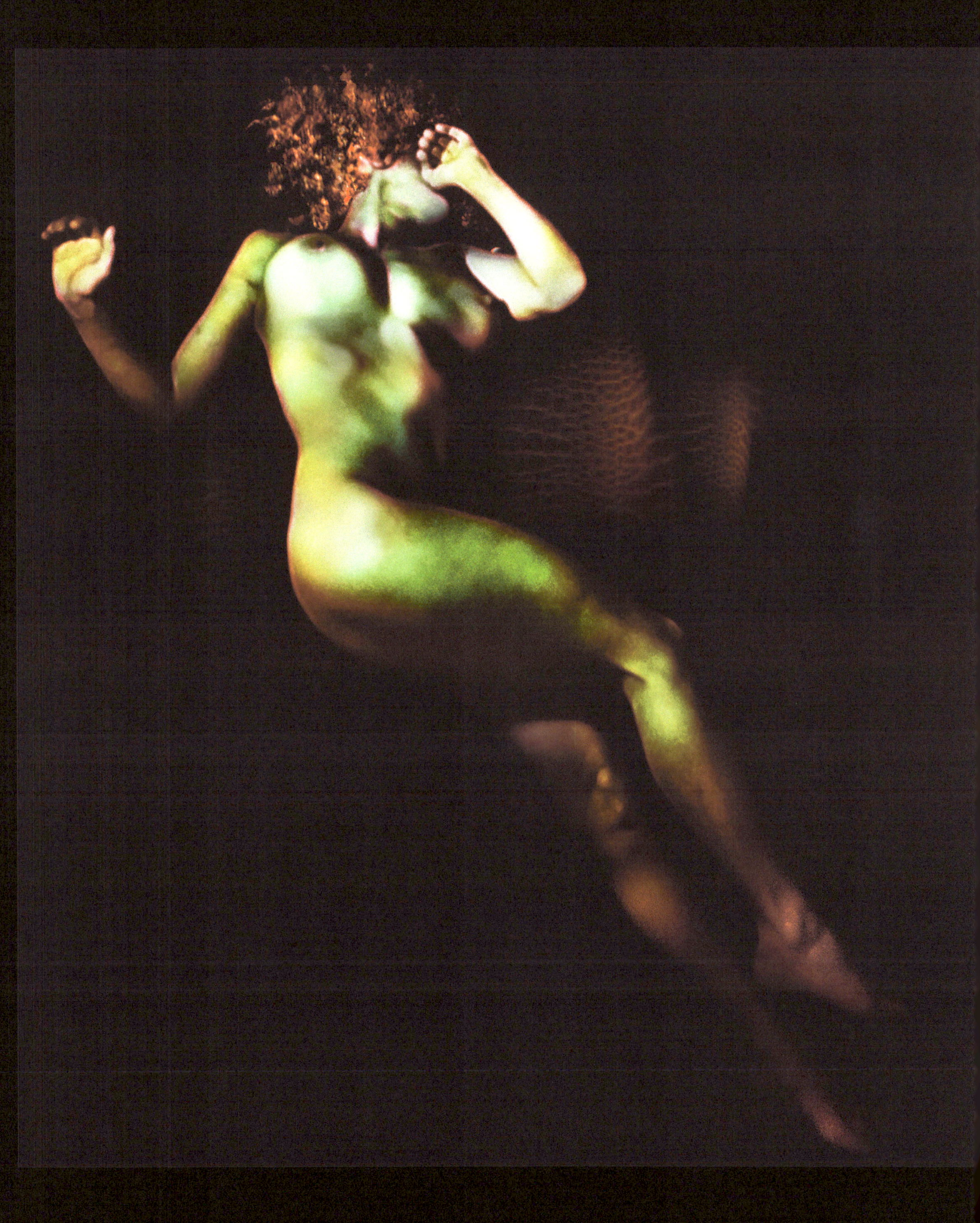

Alexis 2
2008 | digitally enhanced textured photograph.
O.P.S. - 24" x 28"

When the world tilts around you balance is everything.
An invocation of a dream
Hallowed transport of pitch
Woo me into your funk
Your thrust of stars

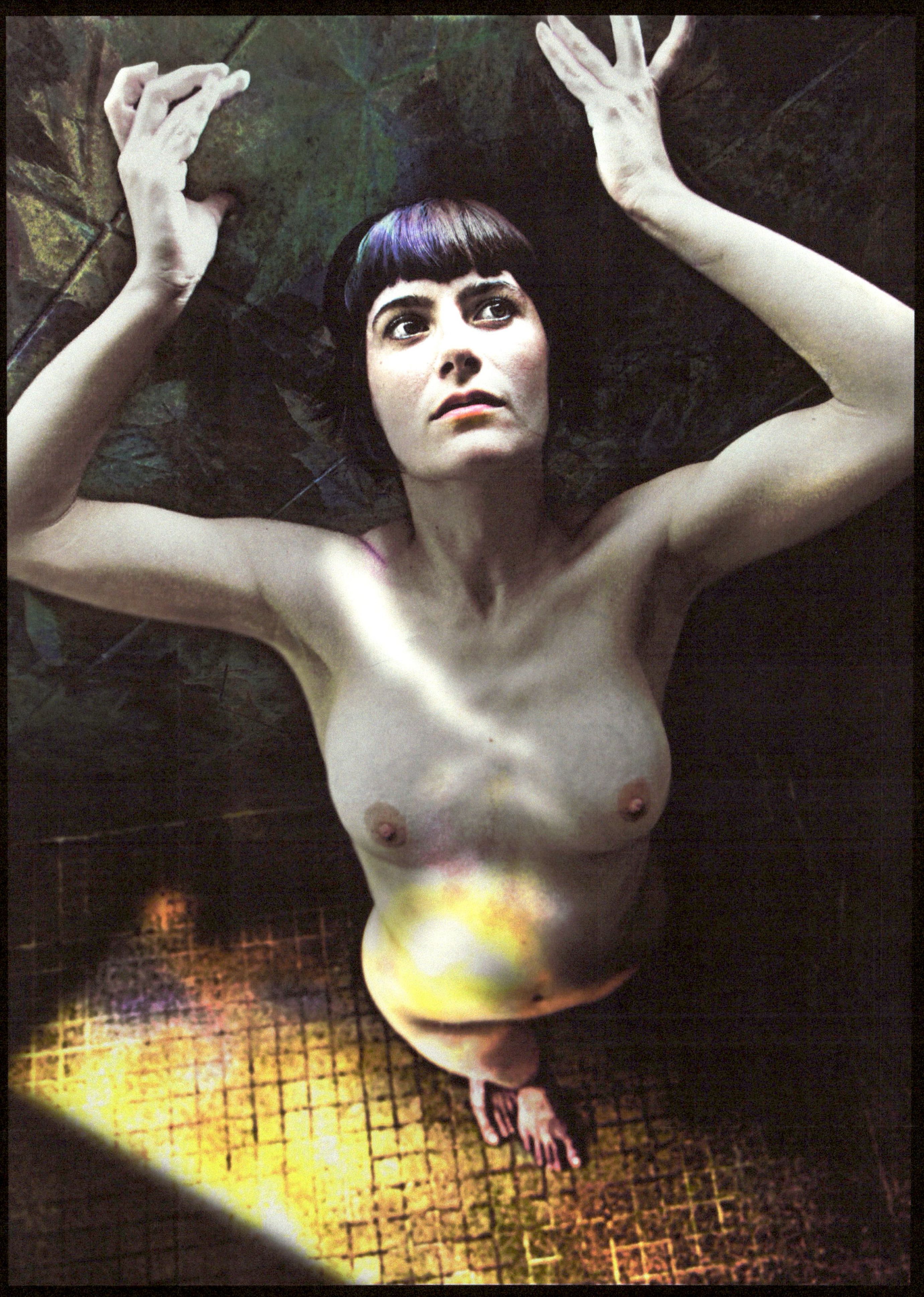

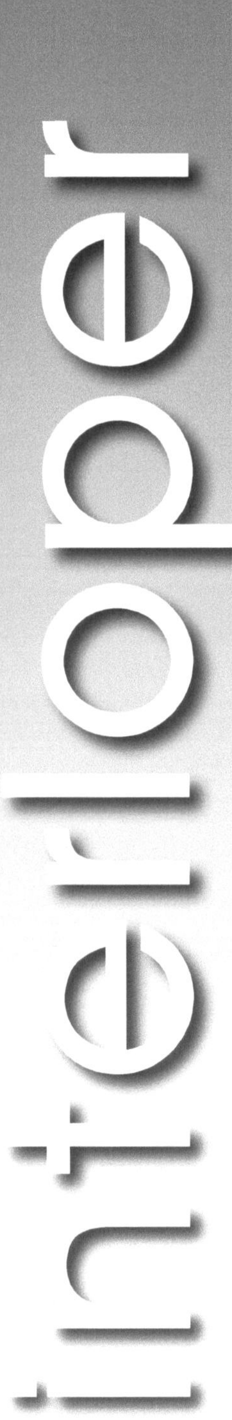

Vespers
2006 | mixed source photo-painting
O.P.S. - 14" x 32"

The width of social continuity
Defined by disheveled beauty
Beyond the usual shadows
Share a vision of intimate blurs

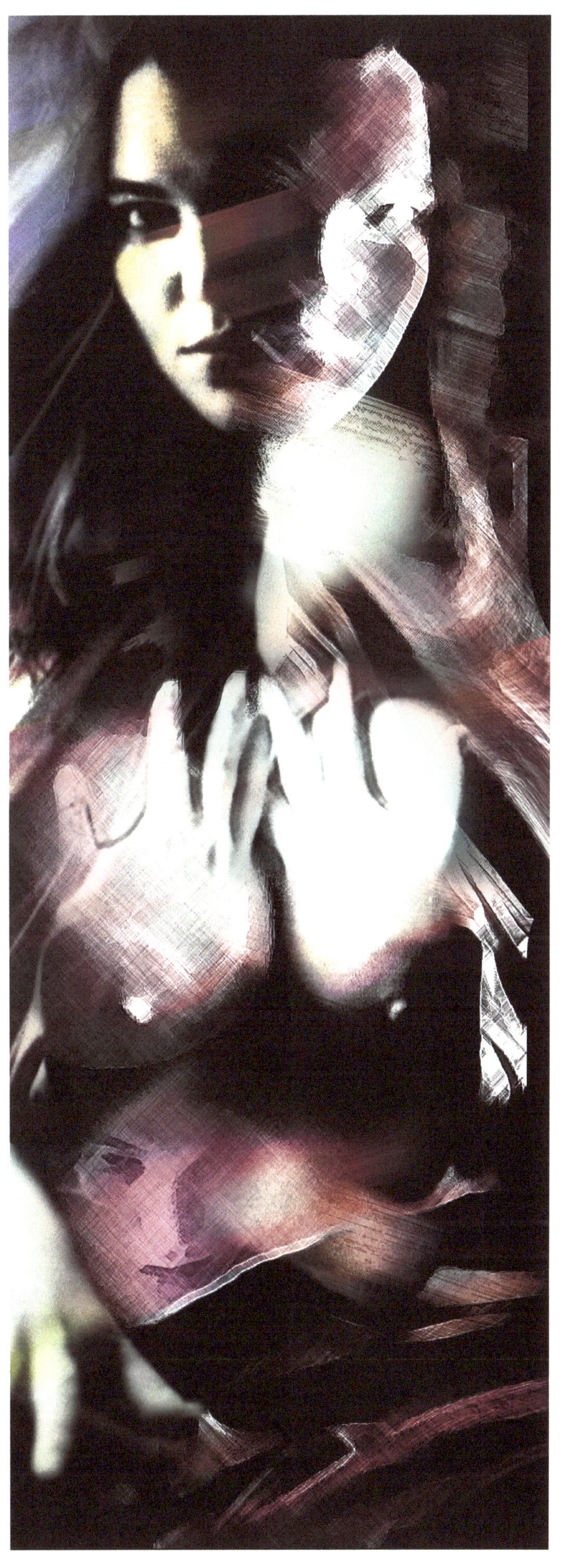

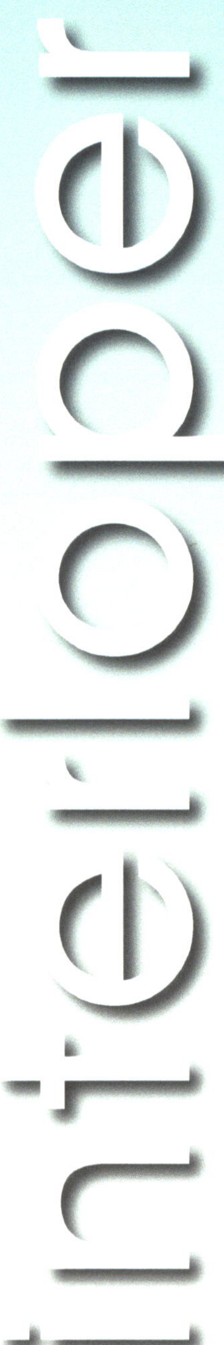

After work
2003 | photo based composition.
O.P.S. - 28" x 42"

What has this magic wrought?
Her Ballerina poised foot consuming her own inertia.
She perceives the passage of blurred tainted breath,
Around now behind, bringing
In bending light,
Her head rotates in dark curiosity, eyes reverse as forward
And backward meld.

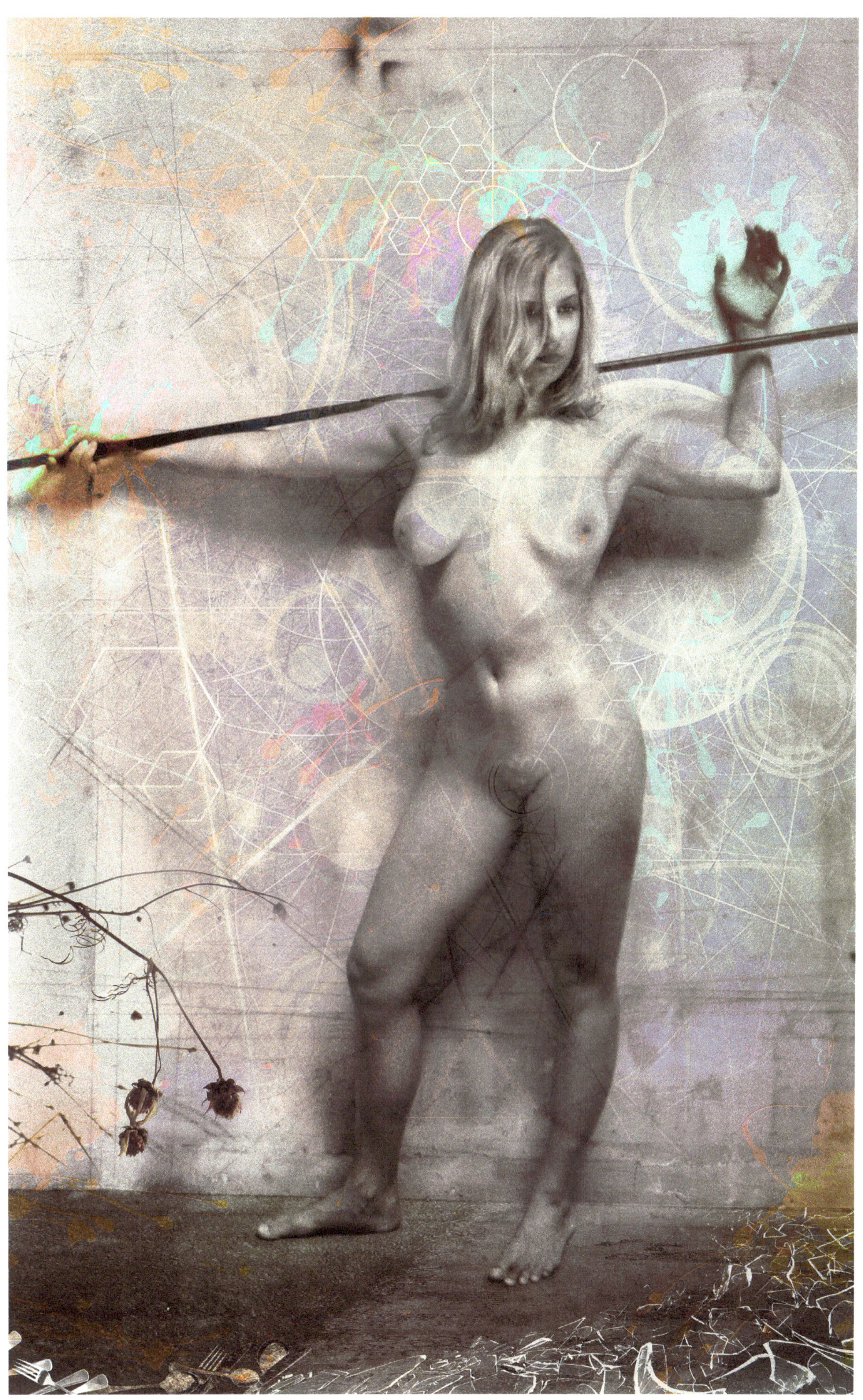

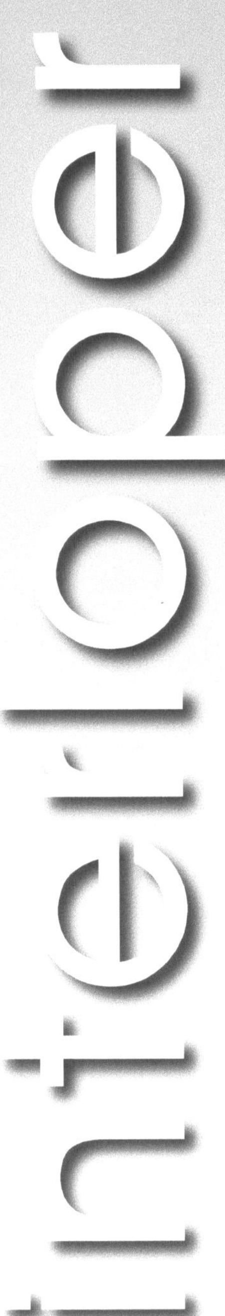

Balloon
2008 | photo based composition
O.P.S. - 48" x 32"

The weight of passion keeps me still and weightless, lack of oxygen killing brain cells, the prisoners escape feeling something. I flail about....nothing.

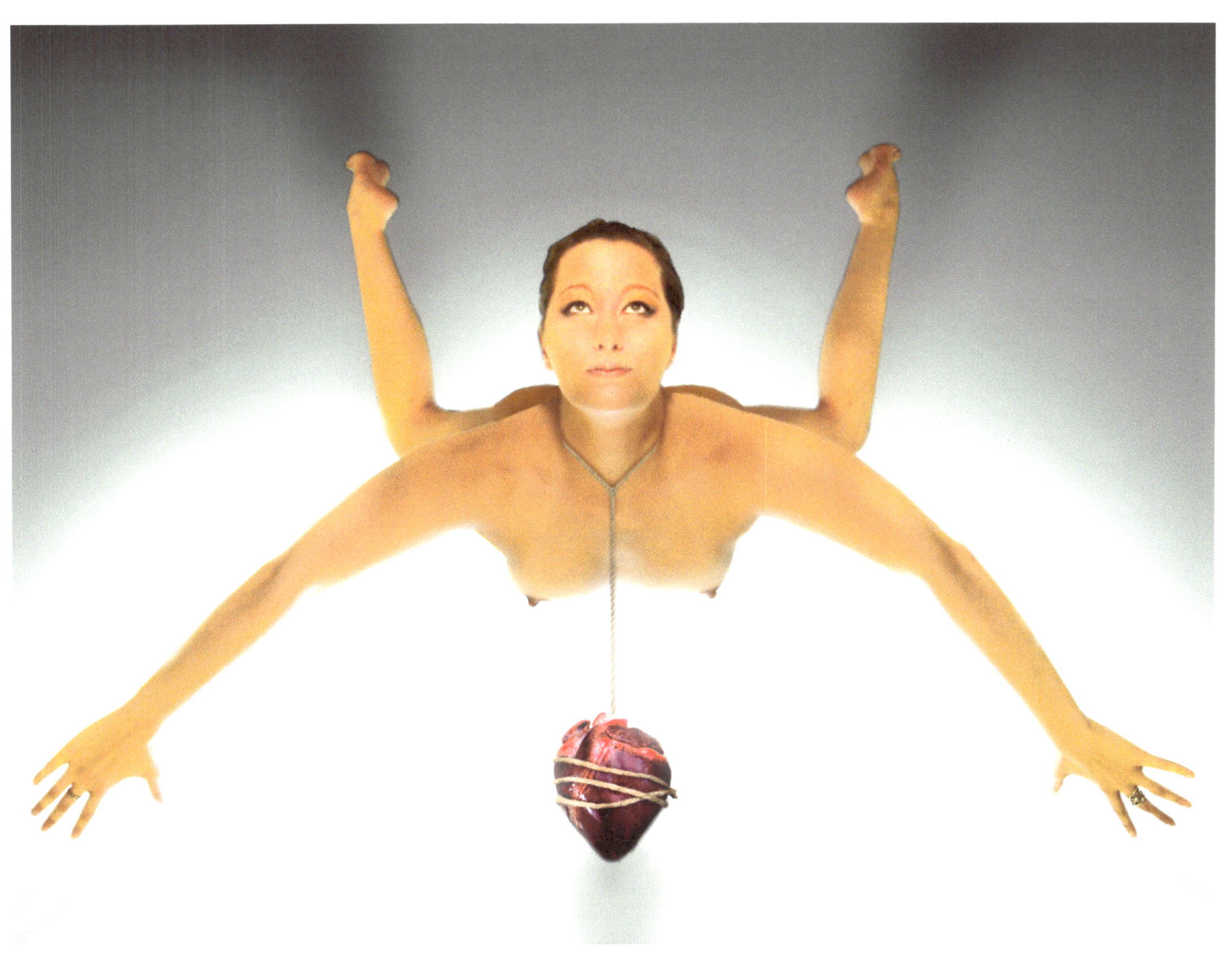

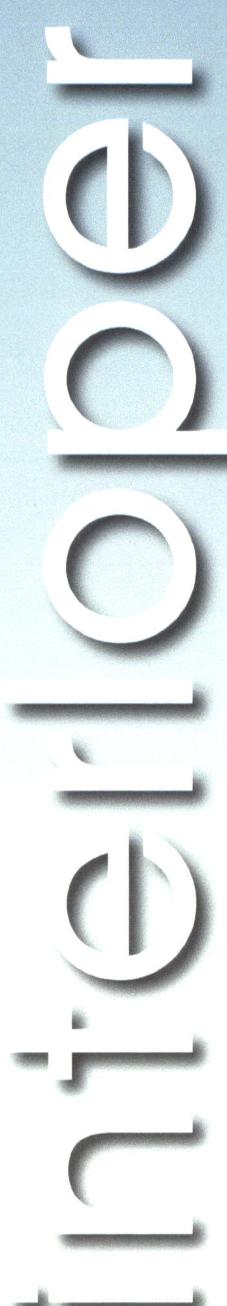

Party on the main line
2009 | mixed source photo-painting
O.P.S. - 24" x 36"

Disciple of knotted hair and dusted angel wing. Kissing tangled sheet and wiry body pale. Sweating heat, straining drug lust abandon in a 1977 summer. Held together by erections imbued with the intensity of a house burning down, set alight by chemical combustion spiraling in slowly opening bloodshot fire eyes. Blink, shudder, still asleep to gravity's spins... throwing myself up.

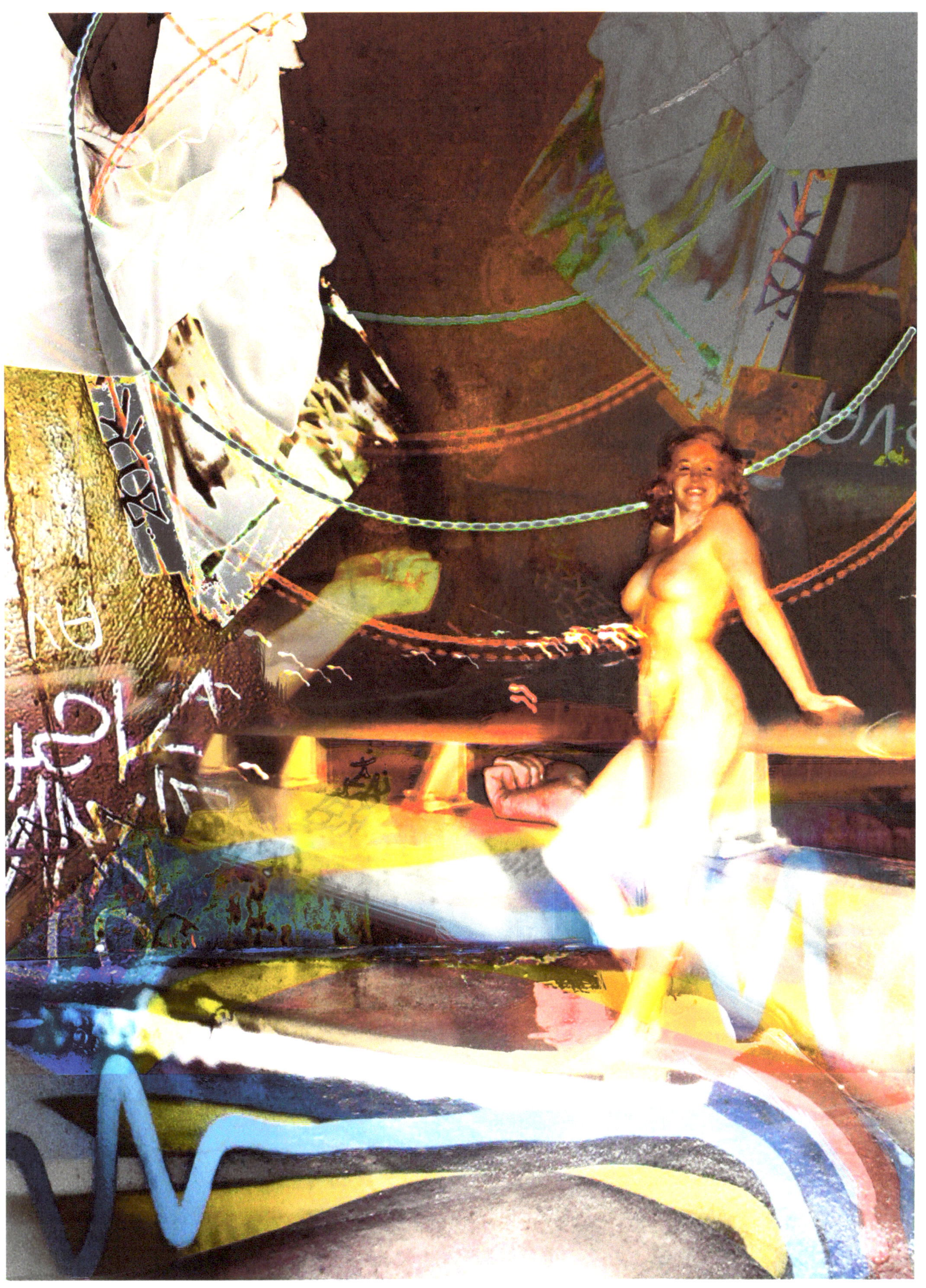

interloper

Afraid of the light
2009 | mixed source photo-painting.
O.P.S. - 24" x 42"

She's rising light, to her feet
And starts uphill through nature's hair
To set herself rolling....
To set herself rolling across heaven again,
Just for the sake of the dizziness of the fall.

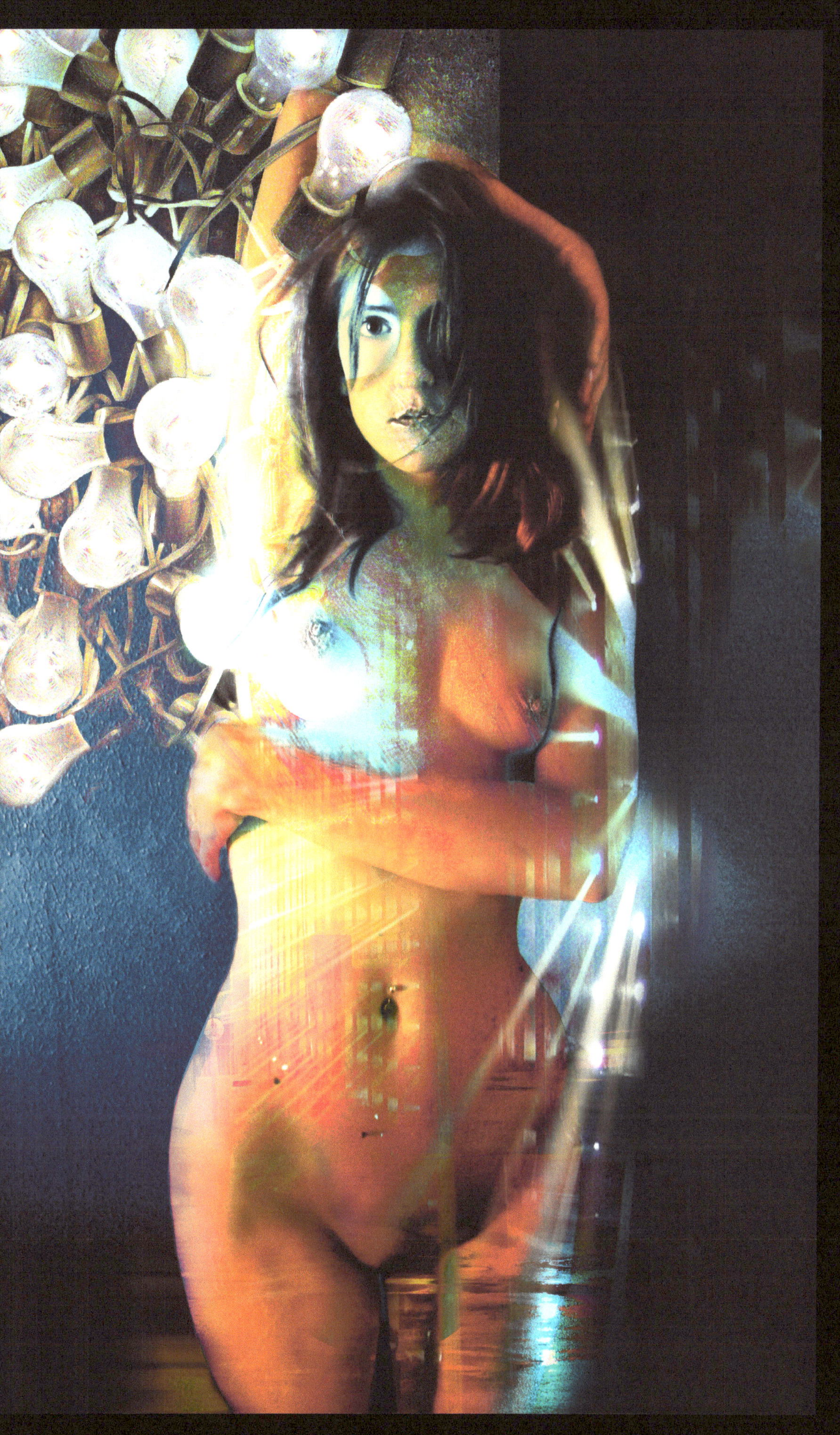

interloper

She's complicated

2008 | mixed source photo-painting
O.P.S. - 20" x 32"

I can't help but wonder if there is ever any sleep

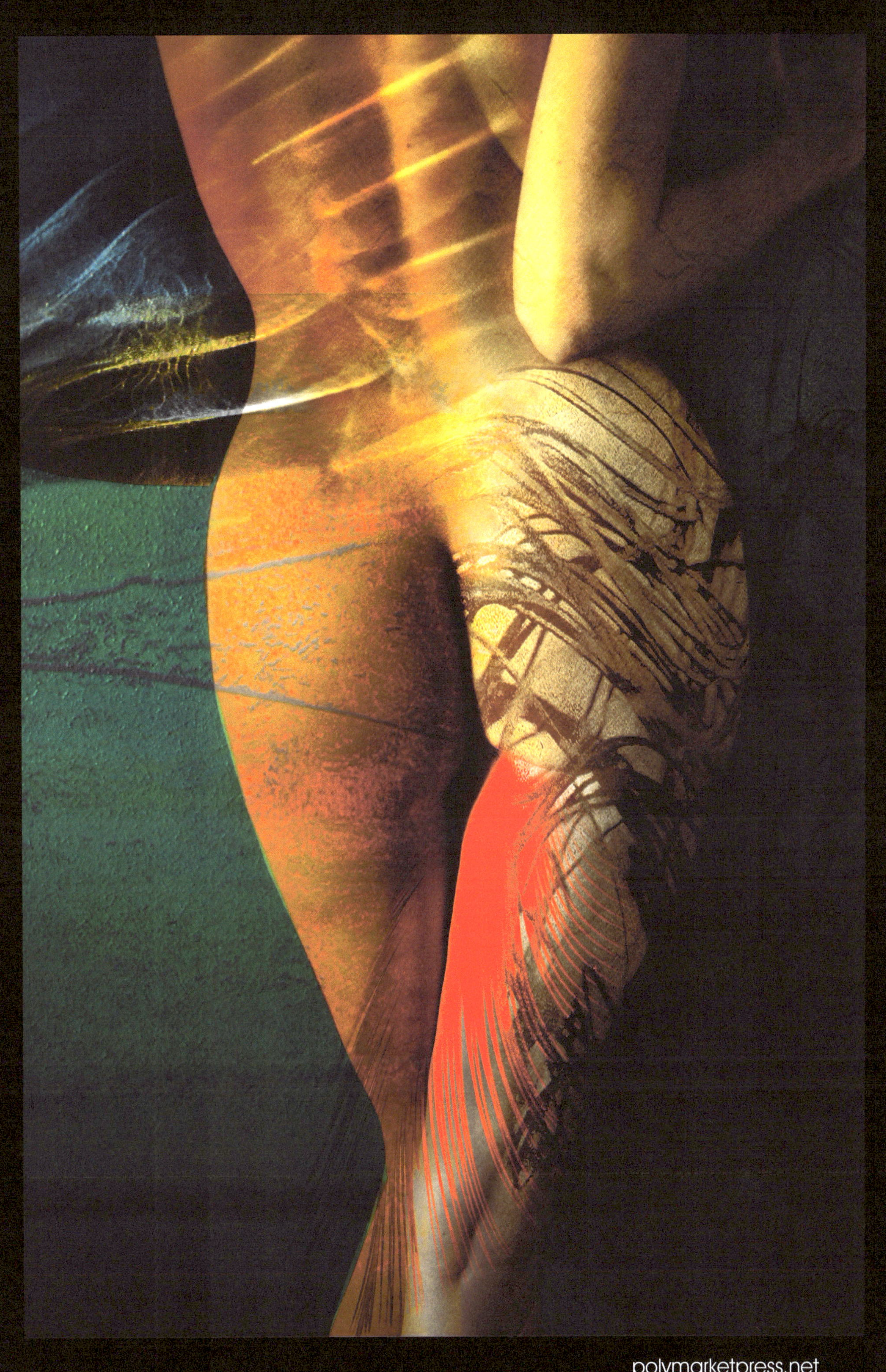

interloper

Mary of New Amsterdam
2009 | mixed source photo-painting
O.P.S. - 24" x 40"

Stretched out on imagination
Racking with the need to grow
Competition of adolescence funneled.
Defining years of men pretending to be
Holy Ghosts
Love rending your nerves exposed
Curiouser and curiouser
Till air seeming too thick to fill you
With any buoyancy other than
That of a bobbing apple in a bucket

Your face is wet...

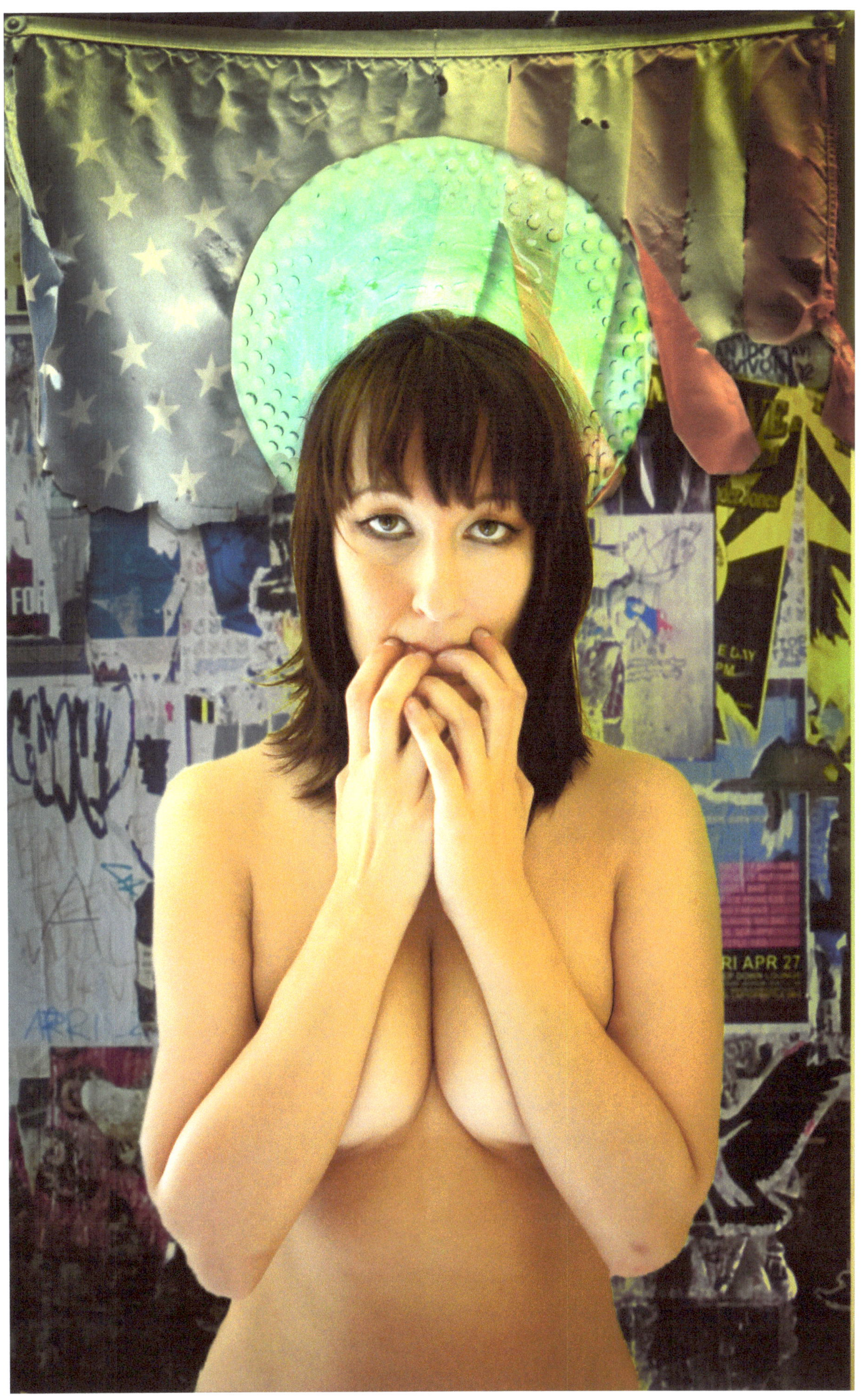
RI APR 27

interloper

1972
2009 | mixed source photo-painting.
O.P.S. - 28" x 42"
Mother country awaits all her dead heros
Little boys play Vietnam with plastic guns and forts of cardboard dance a strange dance of proof. She's across the room jumping into works, falling aspic onto tongues.

(Note: Kent State newspaper headline)

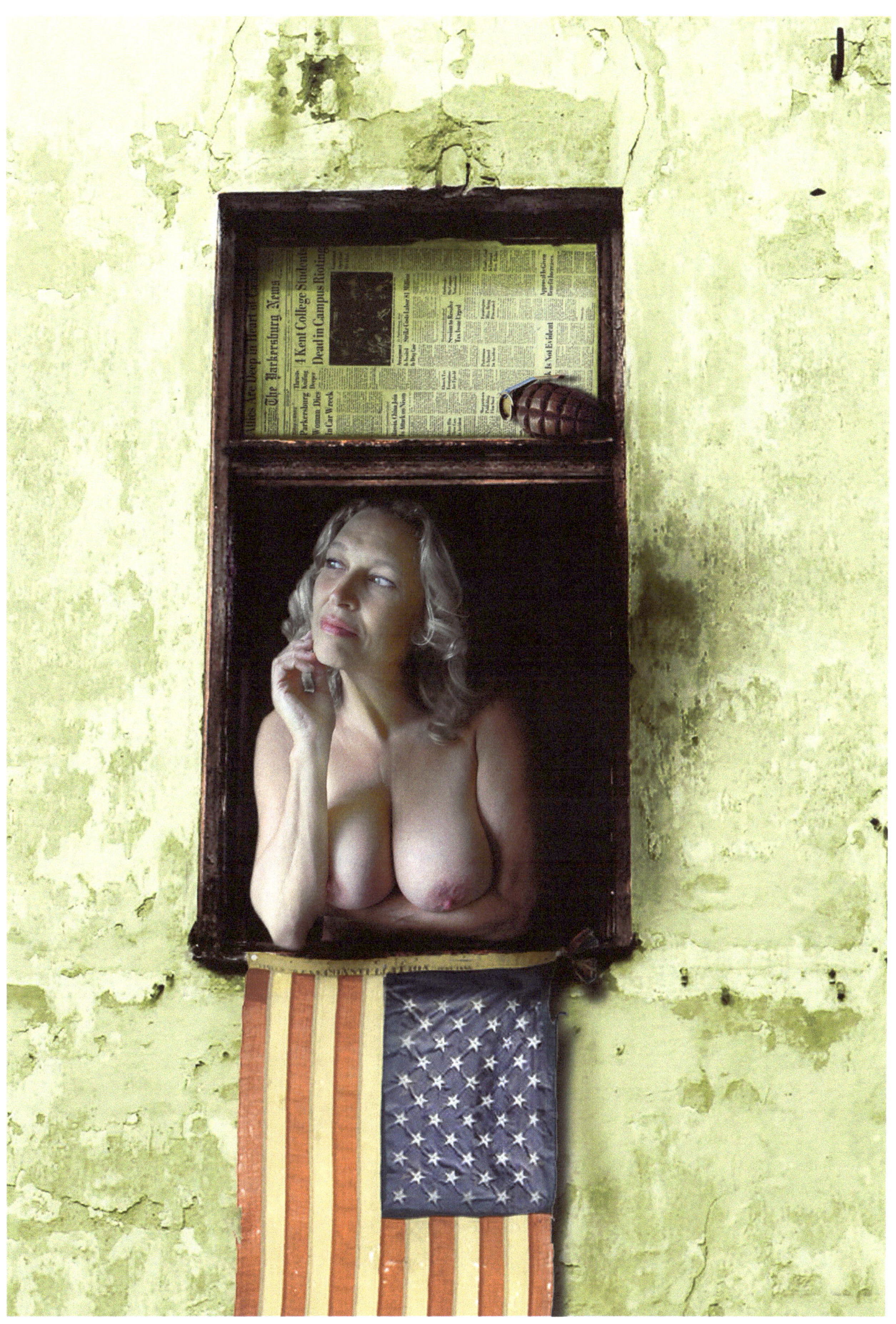
The Parkersburg News
4 Kent College Students Dead in Campus Rioting

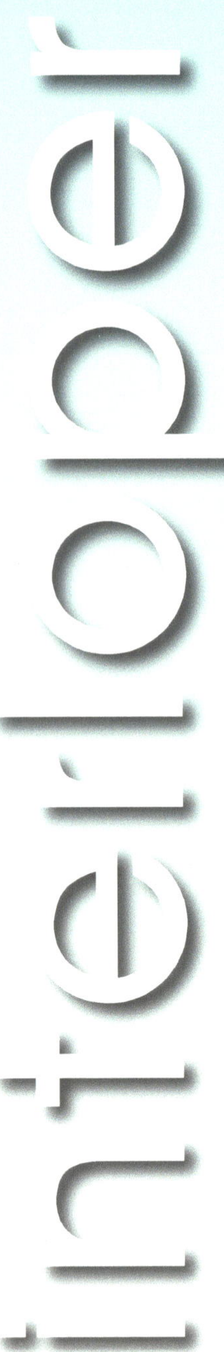

So you think it's hot here

1996/2004 | digitally enhanced textured photograph.
O.P.S. - 36" x48"

All the Earth shall be filled with joy.
Though governments auction prophylactics to black markets
While matchstick baby heads and bellies gaze fly
Into clotted saucer eyes an atomic sun.

Though pearled fat farm children smug in
Cardiovascular disease, T.D.'s and Dodges, discard
Silken filaments of flesh (trembling, pin-boned,
Hard-memoried) on the slick doorsteps of veneered
Strangers.

Though free thinkers, loud speakers, prophets, drummers,
Dreamers are shot and brained on sidewalks, their
Tongues nailed to walls in prisons, disfigured,
Starved, beaten, scorched purple with cattle prods
And though lunatics range freely.

Though tribes are suffocated by a cities fall, falling, fall,
Down numbers loose digits all fingers point in curved air
Roil and blame.

Though in the cramped heart of courts, Liberty, a
Commodity, is traded, bought and sold for those
Who got caught at the wrong time at the wrong place
Dialing the wrong number on the wrong color telephone.

Though trade winds and air currents blow poison fumes
And brown skinned sweat, all filled with anarchistic verve... lash out
Too many voices raised loud, just, thunder with no rain.

And though poets wearily obsess
Incessantly trace quadrants within parameters
Of barren inner landscapes.

There is nothing that you can do
To deny,
Control or prevent it
Eventually
All the earth shall be filled with joy.

And the desert shall blossom as a rose.

(created during the Abu Ghraib scandal)

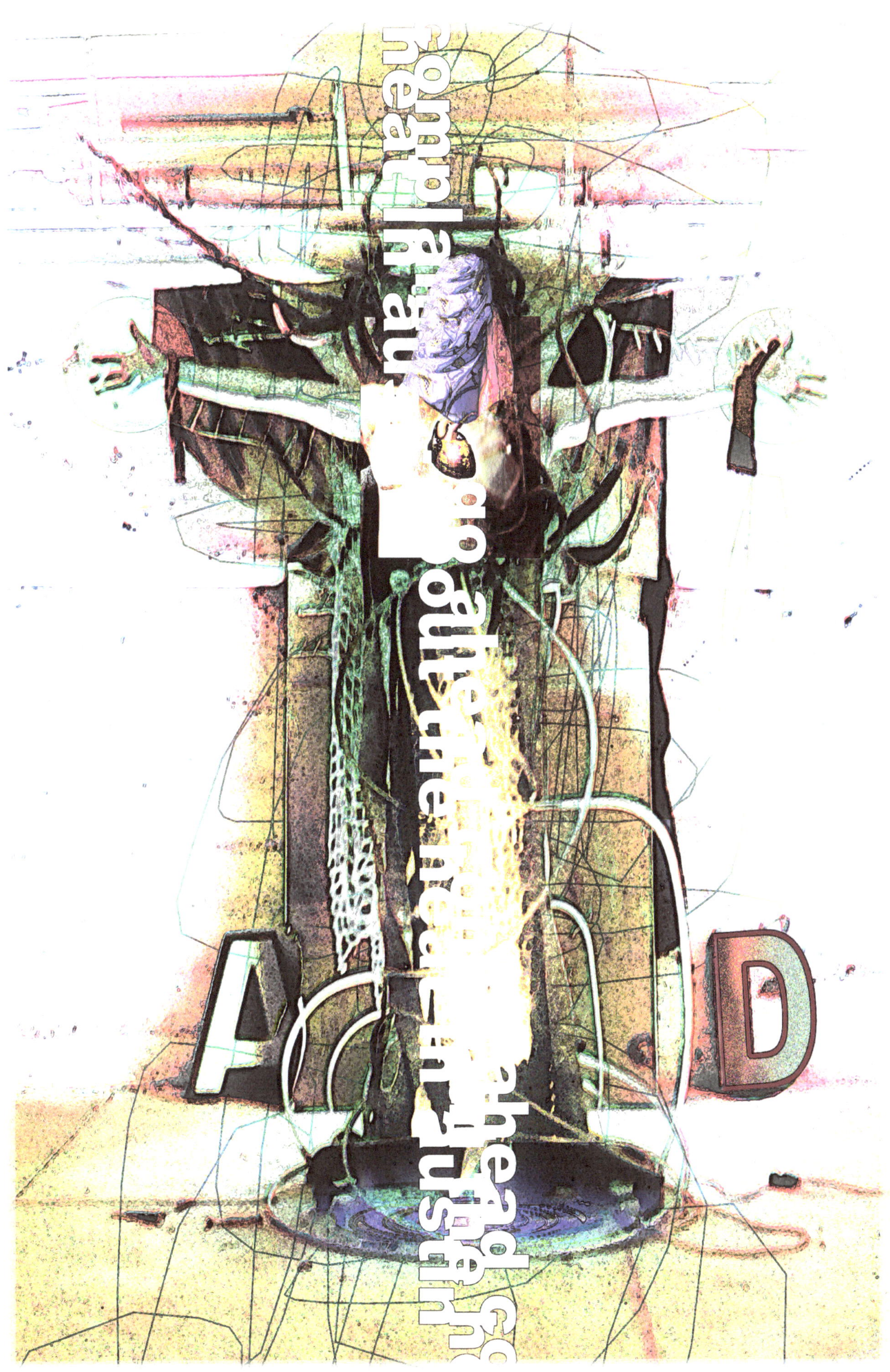
A
D

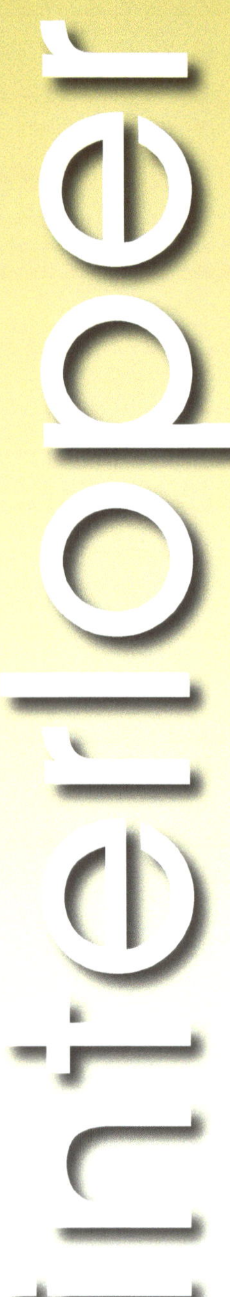

Mrs. America
2009 | mixed source photo-painting
O.P.S. - 48" x 48"

This place you know in your subconscious, your American subconscious, all soft smooth darkness, velvet painting bright, caked garish neon halo Christmas lights left up all year making each day a present to unwrap.

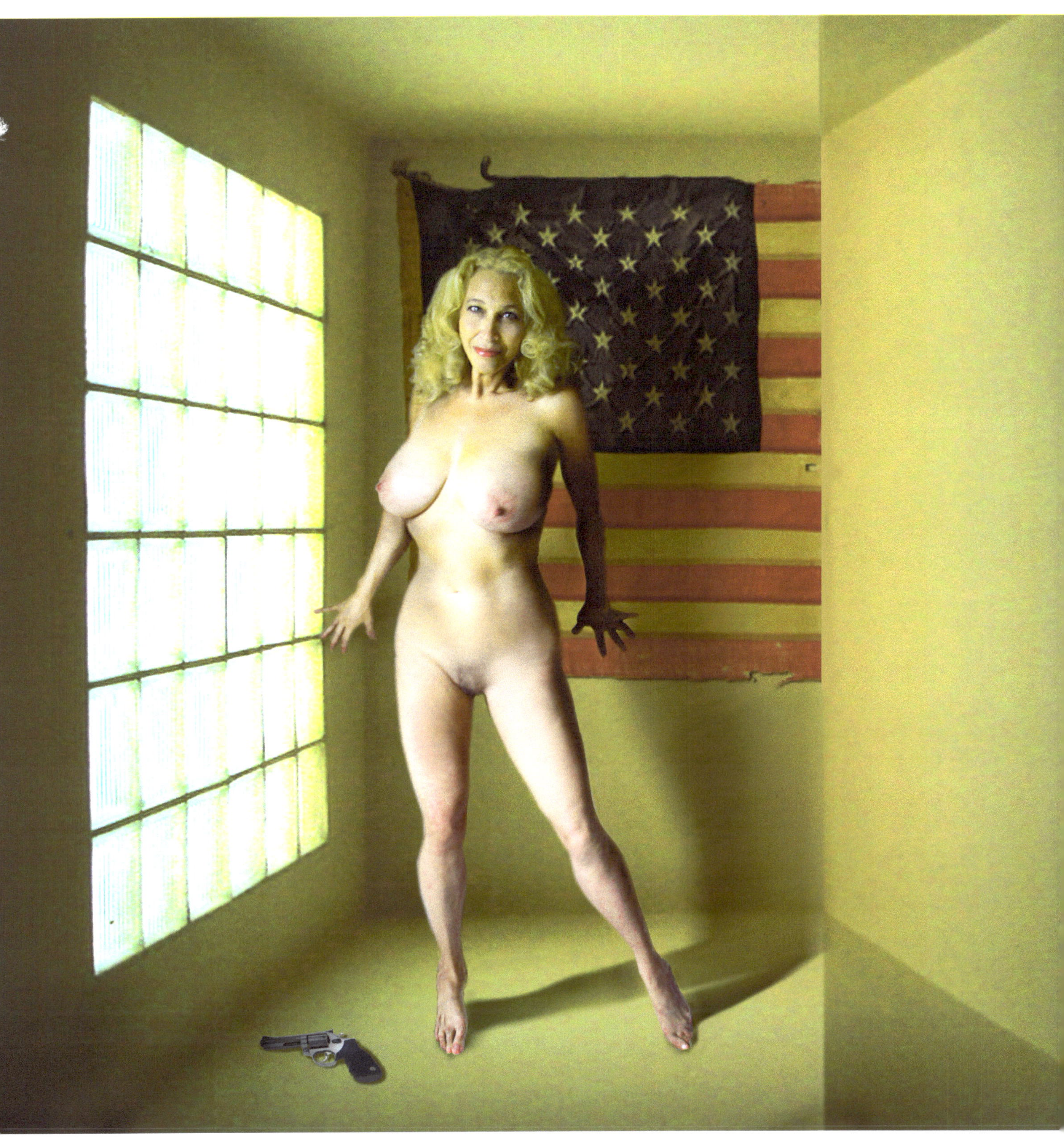

interloper

Somewhere in there
2009 | mixed source photo-painting
O.P.S. - 24" x 32"

Wash it all down
Wash it all down
So clean that it would blind a child seeing his reflection for the very first time. All the evil fascinates, all the good at least amuses. A carnival of distorted faces and pin-cushioned pores.

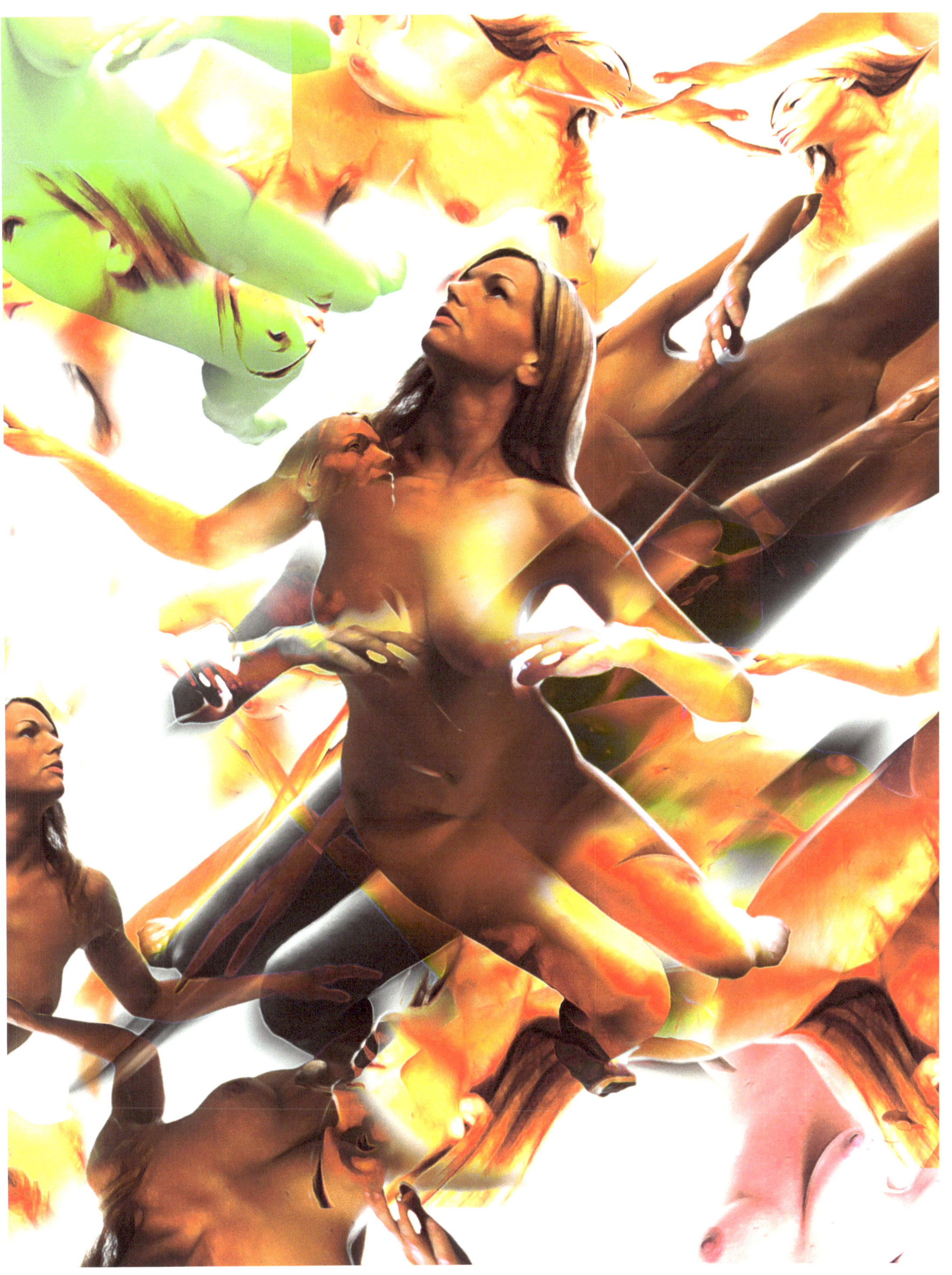

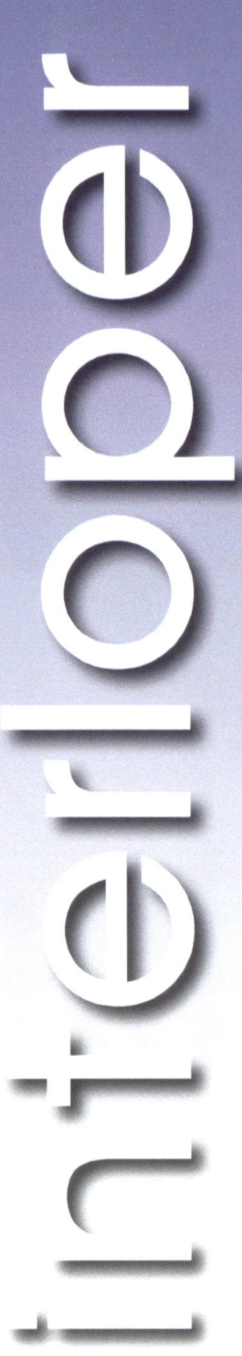

Tempest
2009 | mixed source photo-painting
O.P.S. - 40" x 36"

Waiting here for just a taste of maybe
That ambrosia of opportunity
The lick of slack
And a well measured slap.

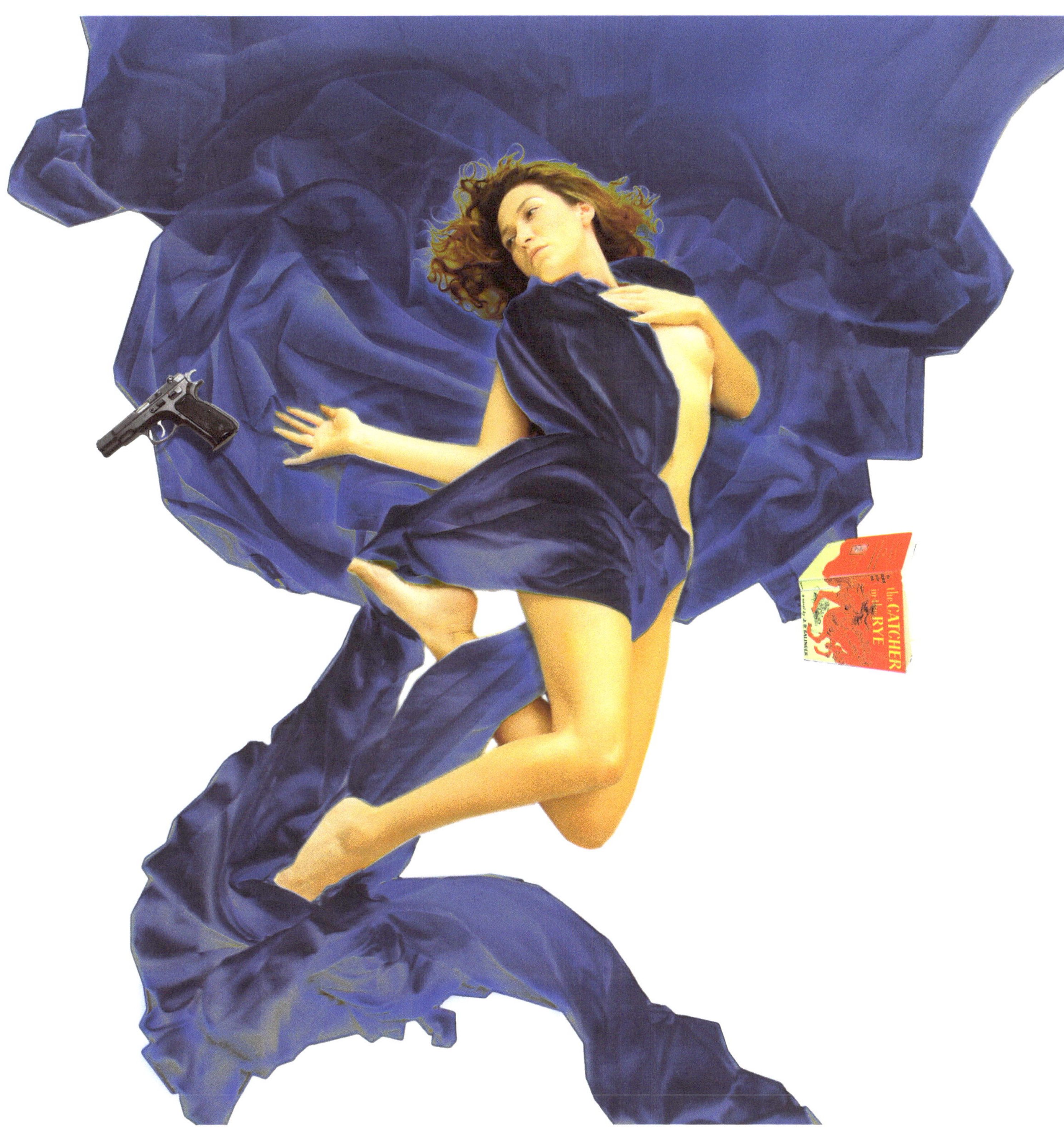
the CATCHER
RYE
J. D. SALINGER

interloper

The cost of entry
2010 | mixed source photo-painting
O.P.S. 24" x 26"

This true blatant wit-man dogma barking in the yard you measure your reassurance with these born of grass stained knees looking back to voiceless answers and blank marked stairs rising up to the heaven examined out of all love. "Hey, my folks are show people, your folks are show people! Lets put on a show!"

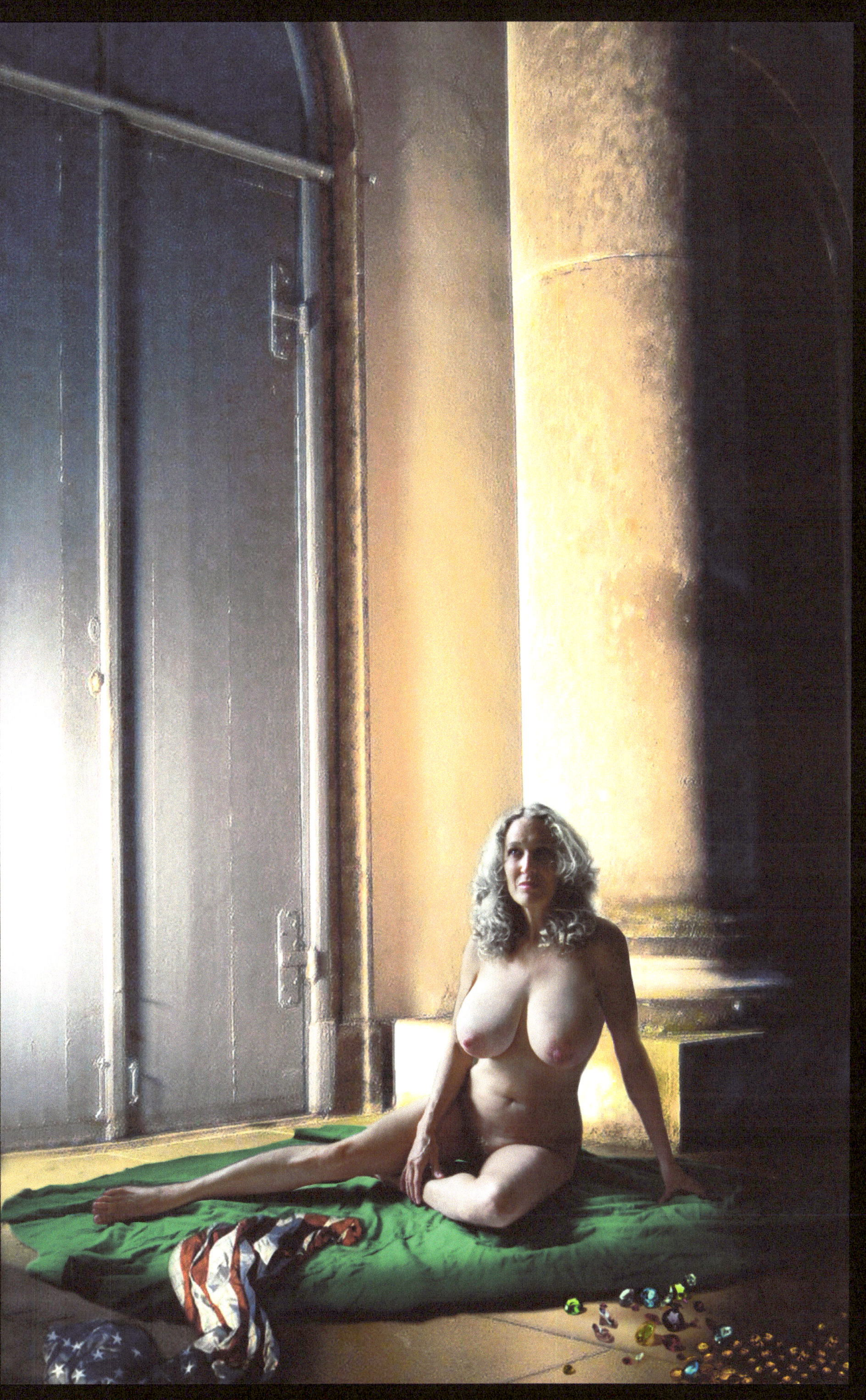

Woe
2008 | mixed source photo-painting
O.P.S. - 24" x 32"

Load of red swirl black history
Preacher juke box talks about
Cultural resisters

Push pin sins - Trance sisters
Translate a torch burn grip
Monster man, Nam monster

Ethical bicycle ridden into
The underground to sleep with
The dead

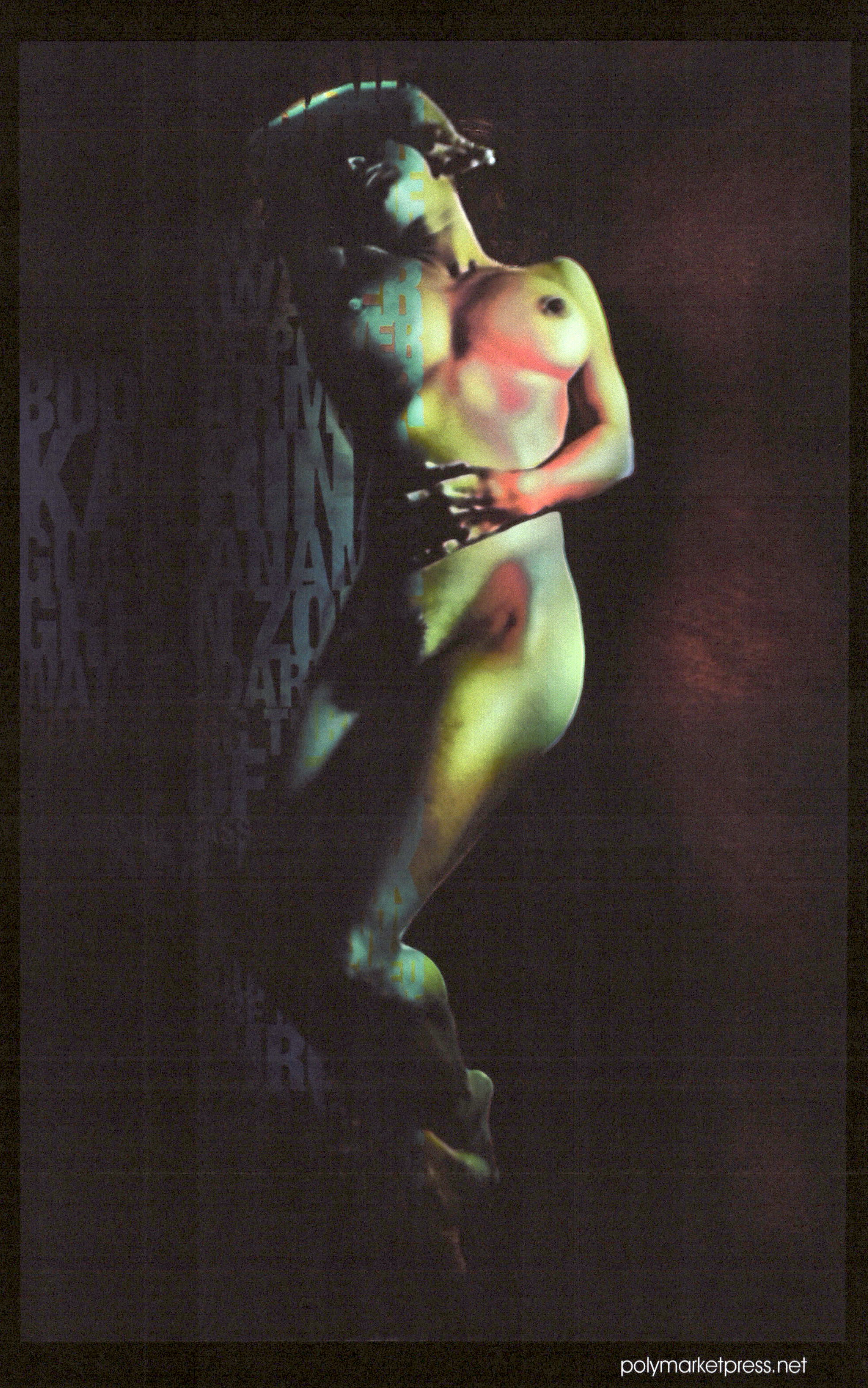

interloper

Writhe
2004 | digitally enhanced, colorized photograph
O.P.S. - 18" x 36"

If I touched you, would you notice?

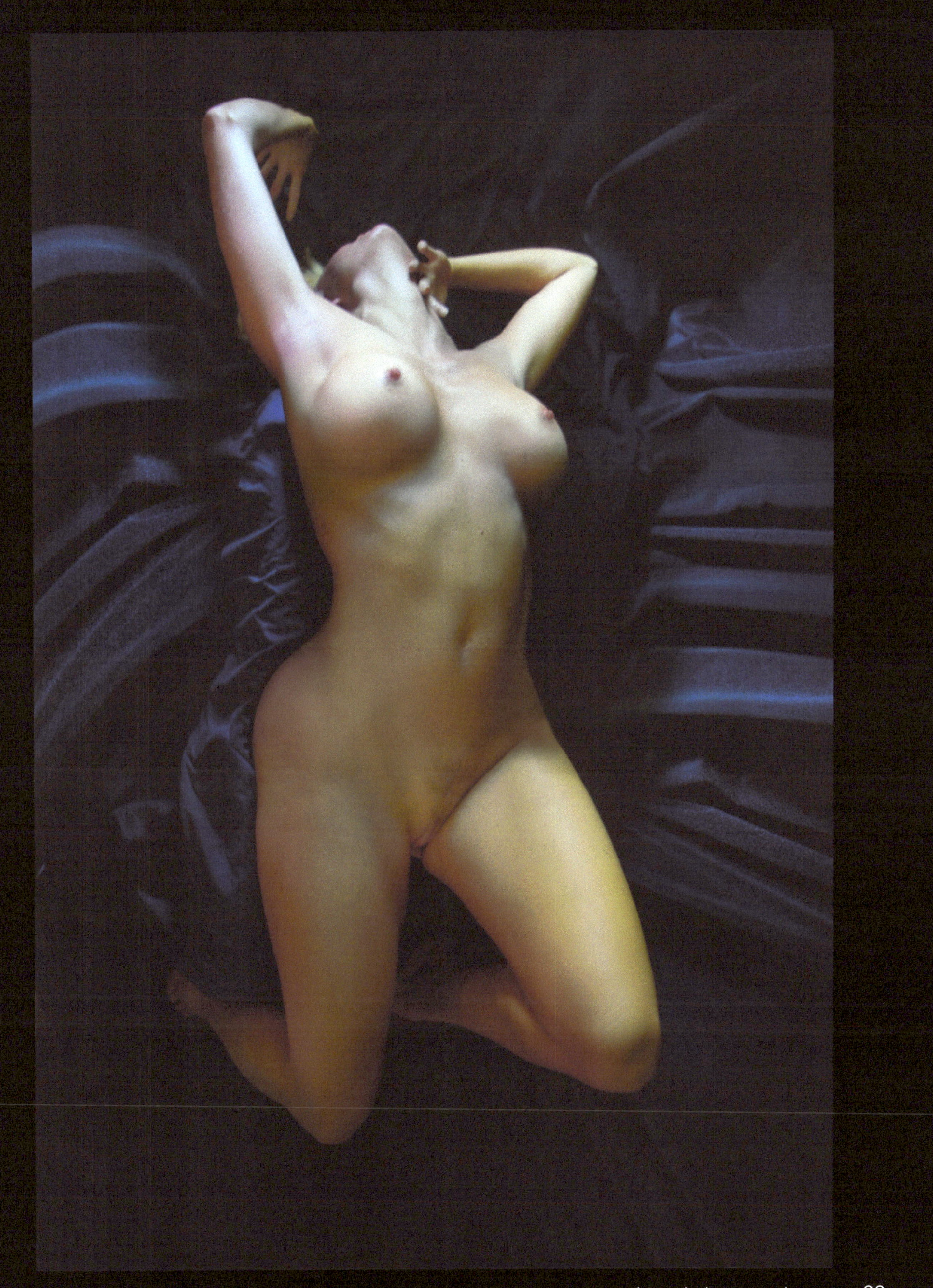

interloper

Note for note

2010 | mixed source photo-painting
O.P.S. - 16"x 36"

The triumph of nostalgia
Better times
Not as they are, as we think they are
Escapes as a ghost.

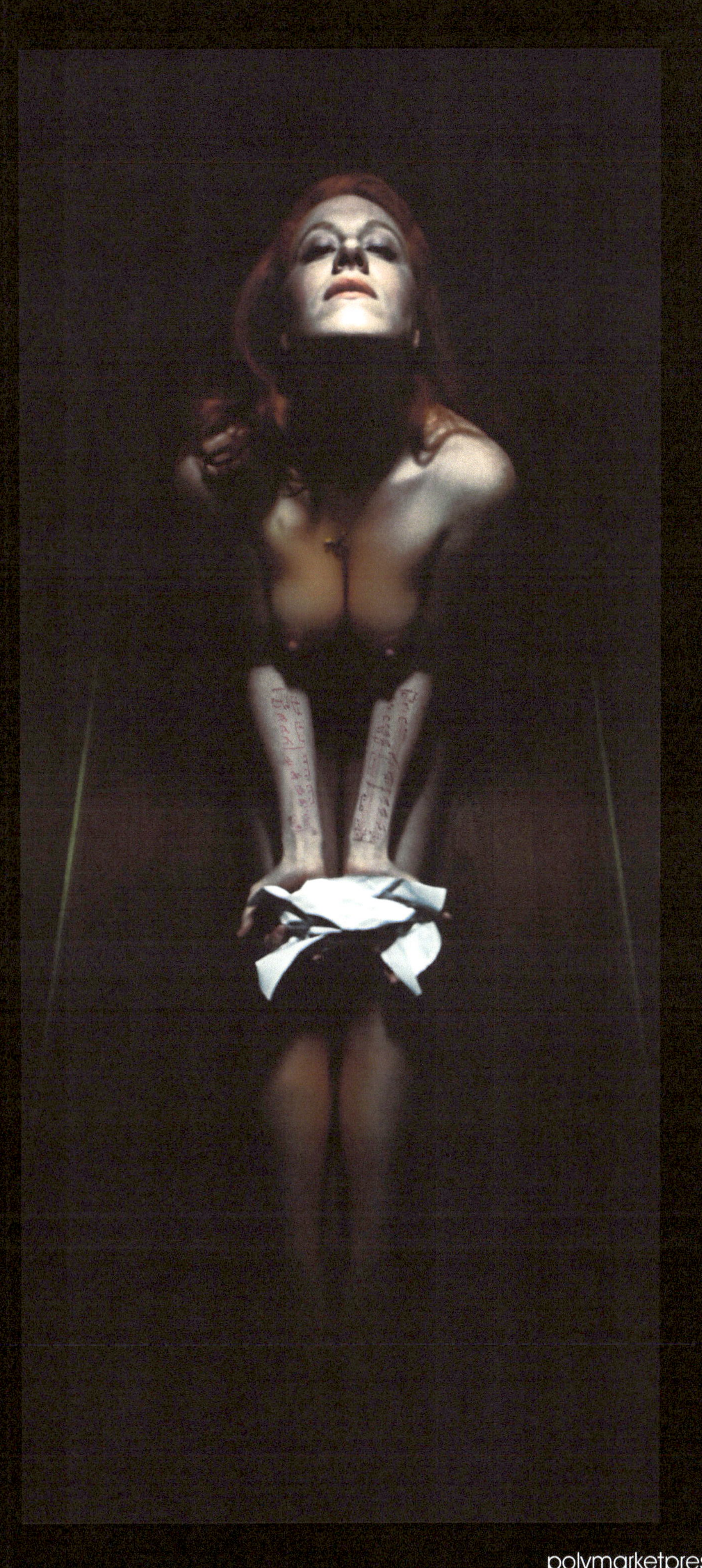

interloper

The phone in the other room

2009 | mixed source photo-painting
O.P.S. - 32" x 48"

Close to me is vague
Not clear is the way I like it
Loud screaming boys in my subconscious
Never growing out of a growl
And on the phone
A cacophony of voices
A poly rhythmic shroud
Large female shaped bass lines
Beat percolates coffee black
Burning a tongue awake.

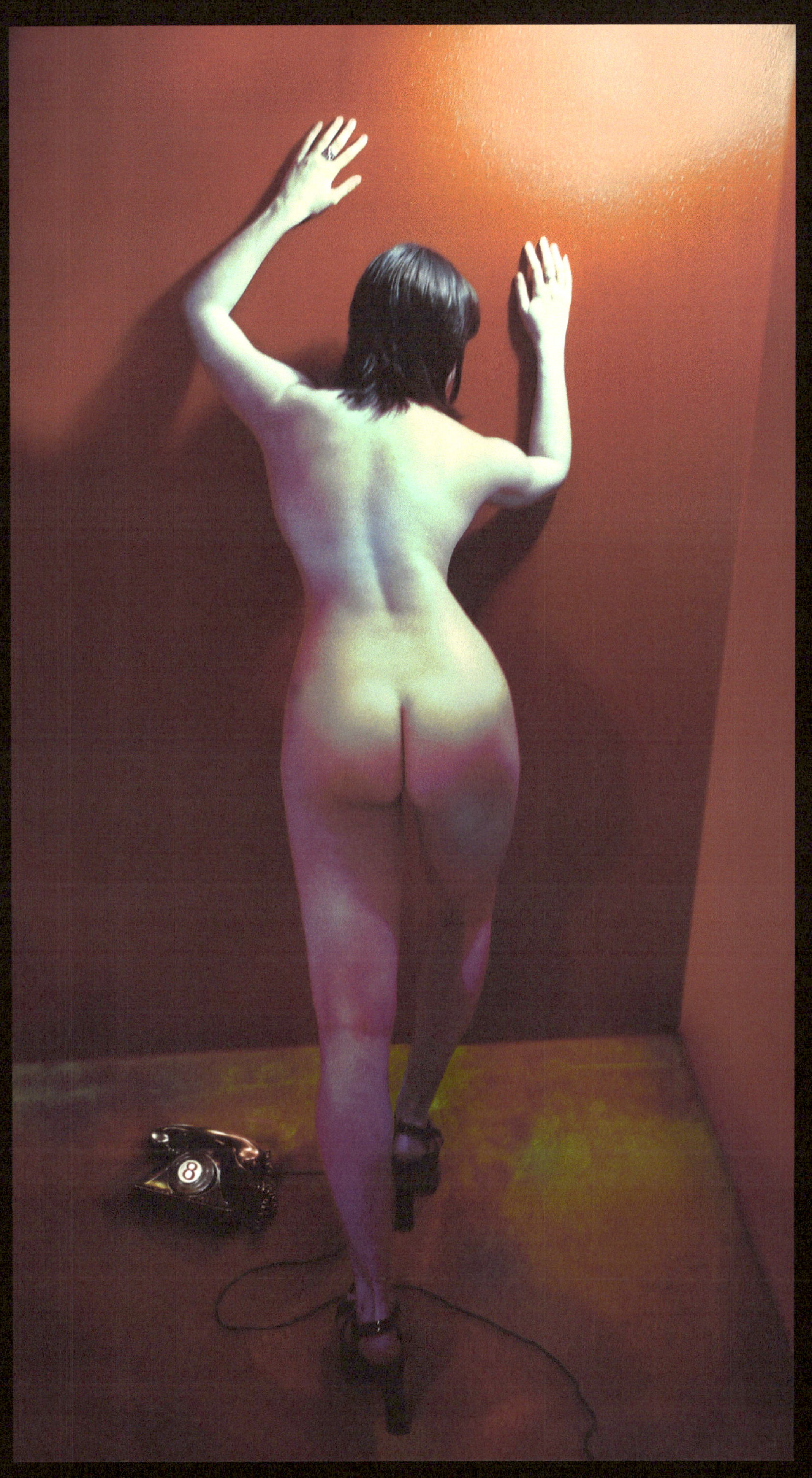

Smoking area
1996 | photograph based, mixed source photo-painting
O.P.S. - 12" x 19"

"Hi"

"Higher than I wanna be"

(Static balloon hanging on the wall)

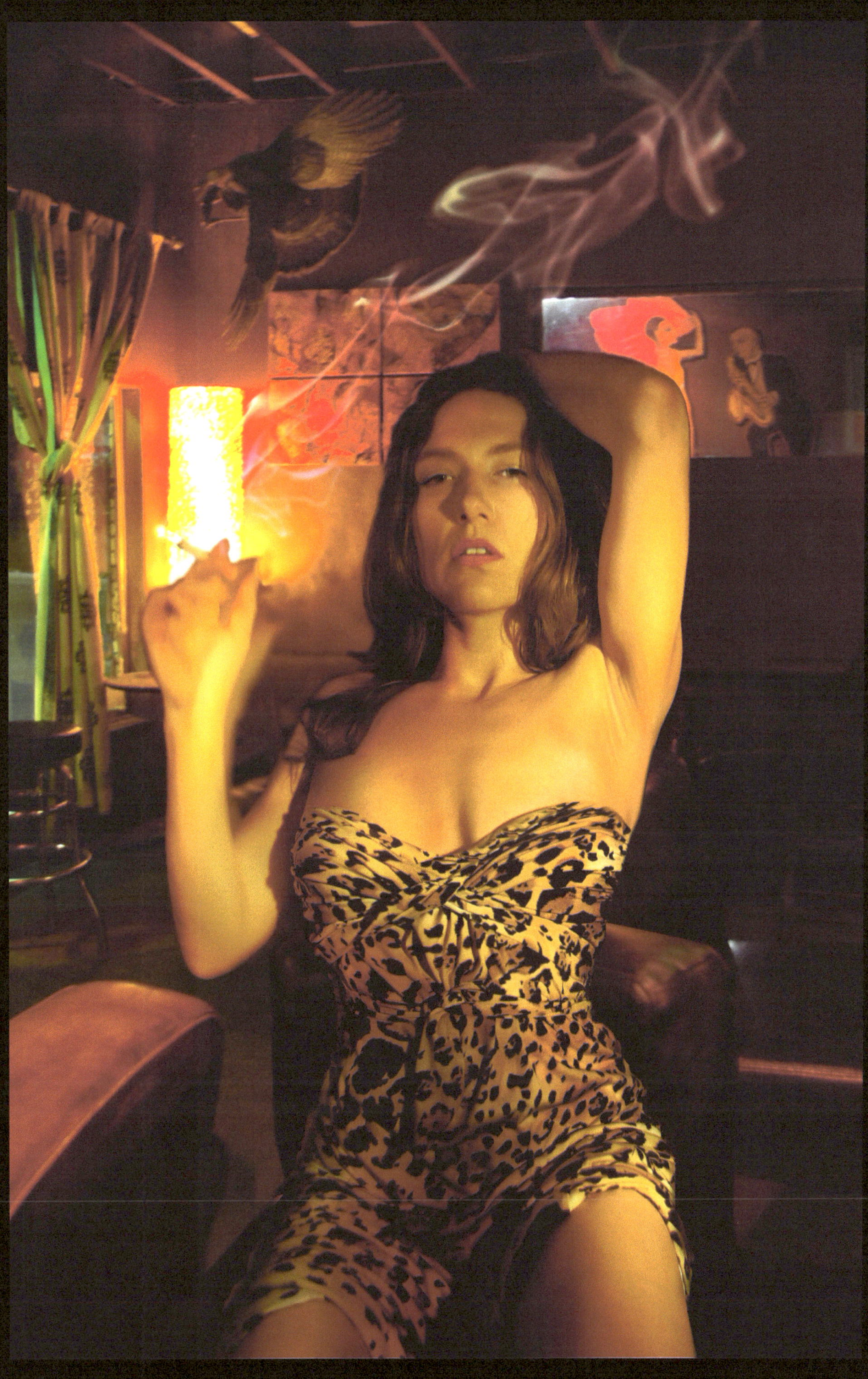

interloper

The corridor
2009 | mixed source photo-painting
O.P.S. - 48" x 32"

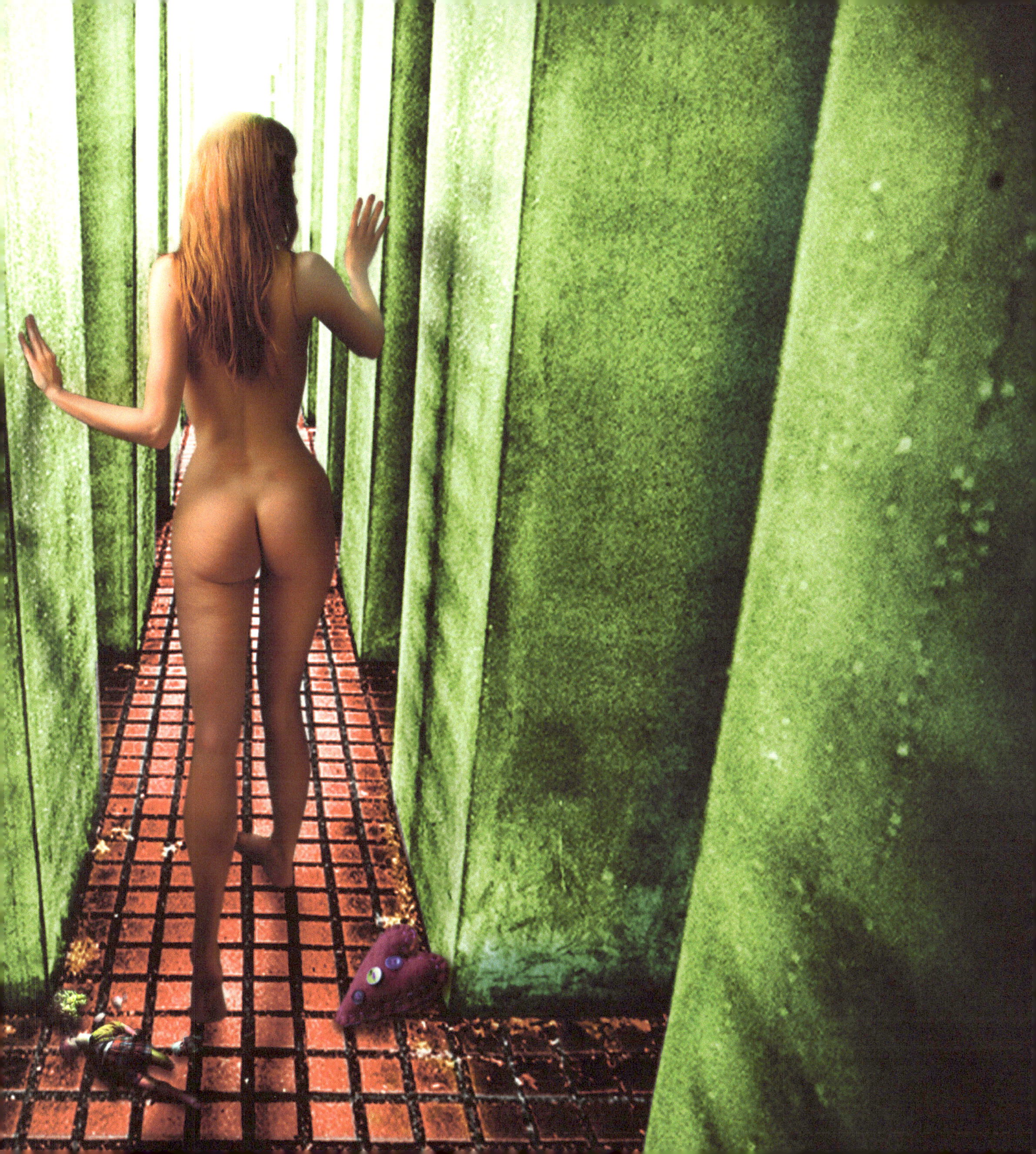

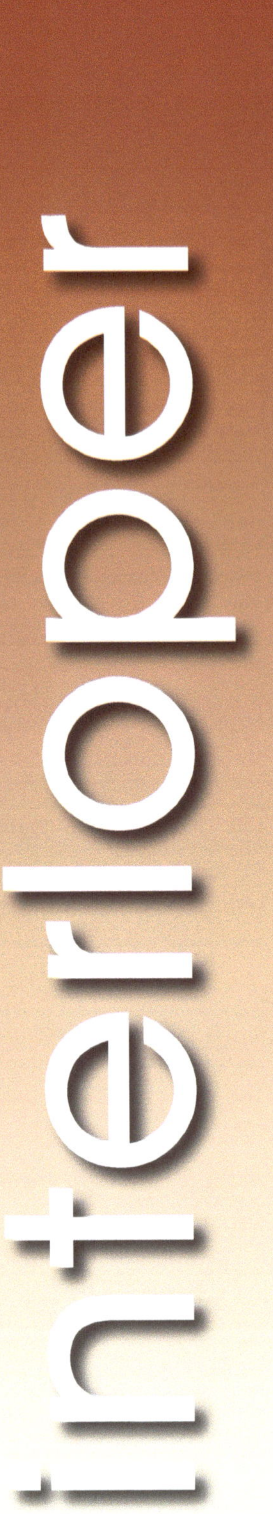

She got out of those bloody things
2009 | photo based composition
O.P.S. - 13" x 17"

The dropping of water on a box of tin
Will keep tapping, tapping, till it finally gets in

Open the window let the rain on in
It will burst to steam
As it hits our skin

The slickness of souls like you and I
Here for a return performance on the sly

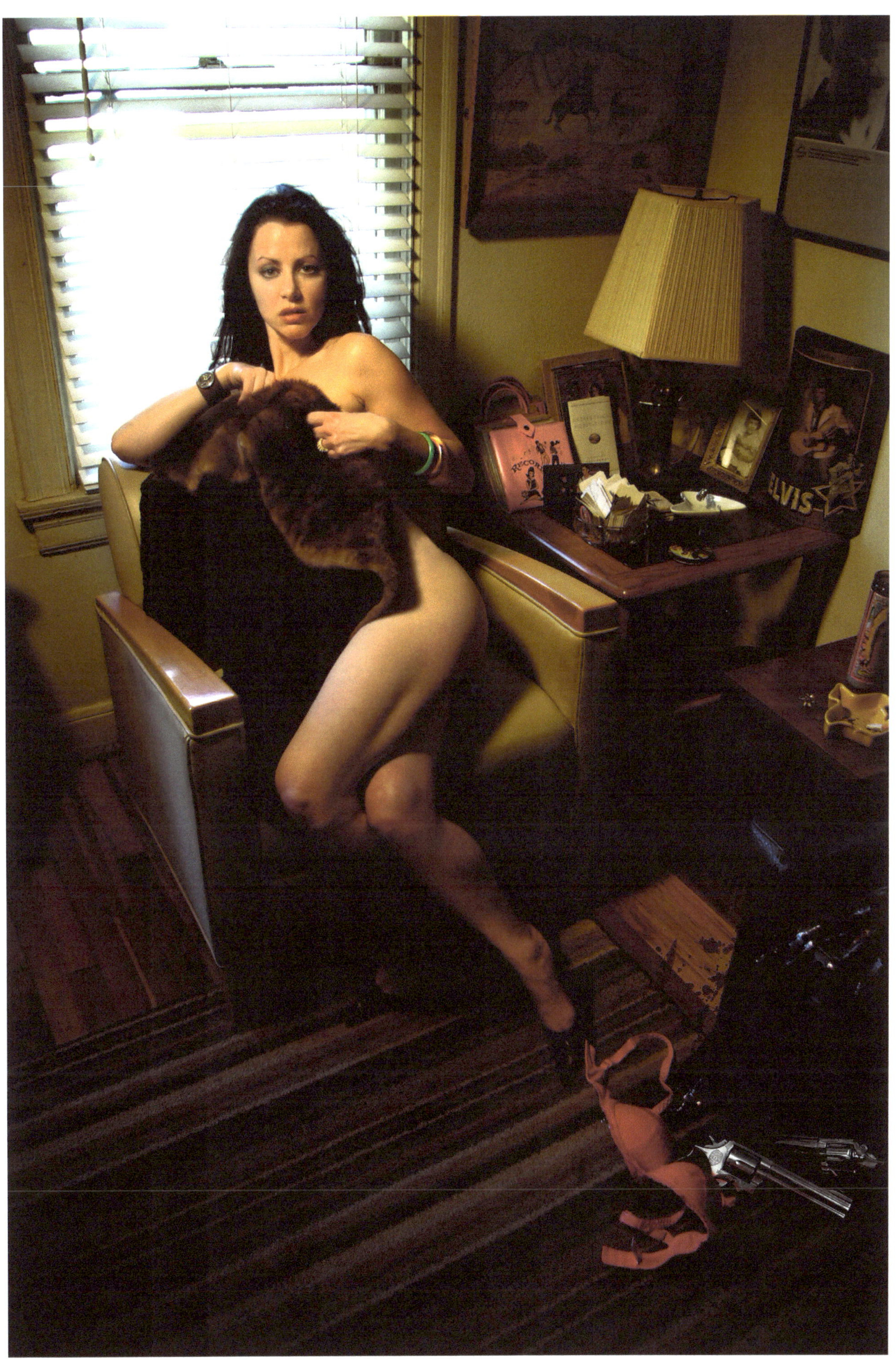
ELVIS

interloper

He won't be breaking anymore hearts tonight
2009 | photo based composition.
O.P.S. - 42" x 32"

Poe does film noir. At some point I've heard it said the heart becomes a hunter, the flesh and sinew take on the role of compass.

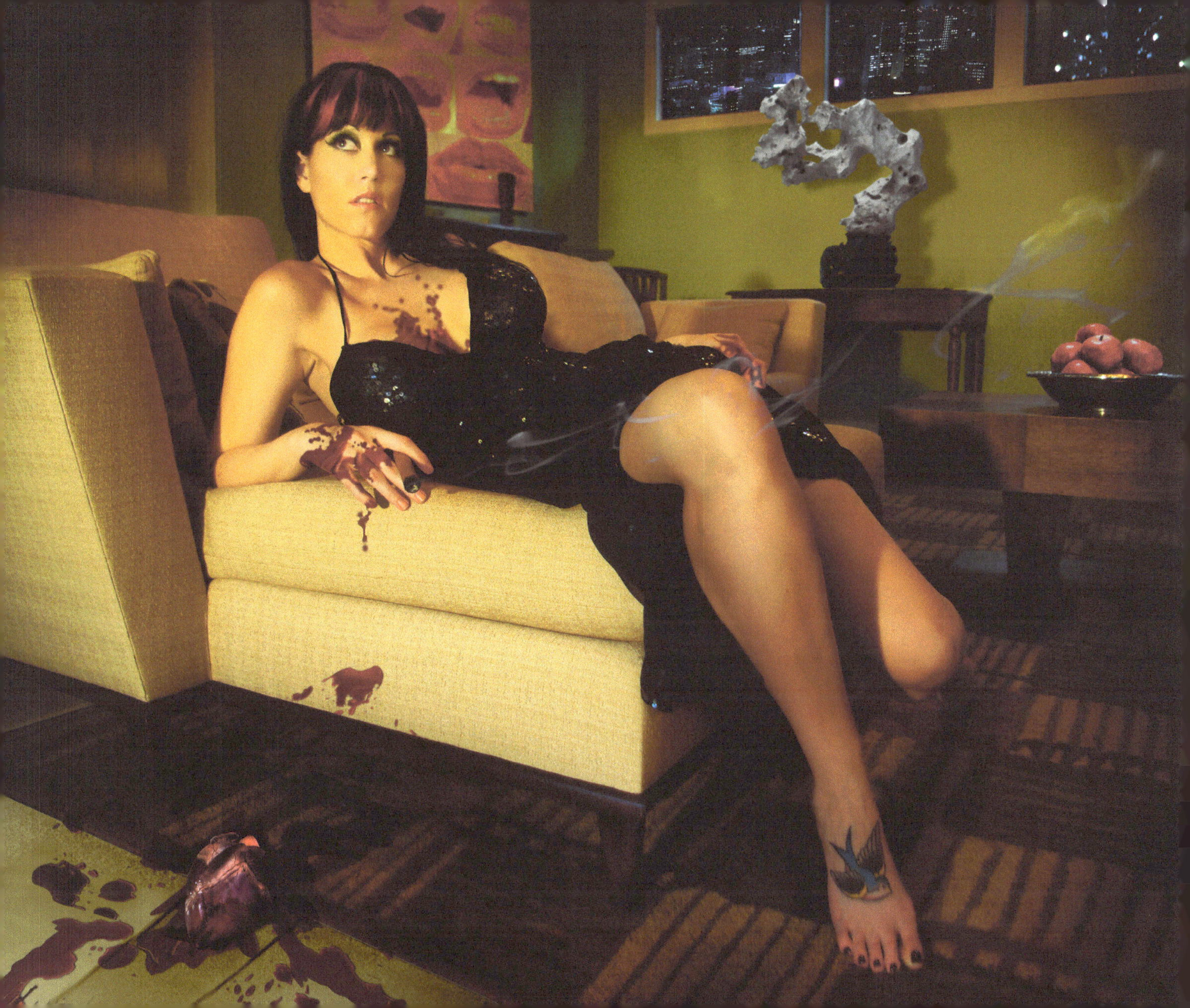

interloper

Hands & feet
1995 | colorized B/W photo
O.P.S. - 36" x 14"

Index of Models

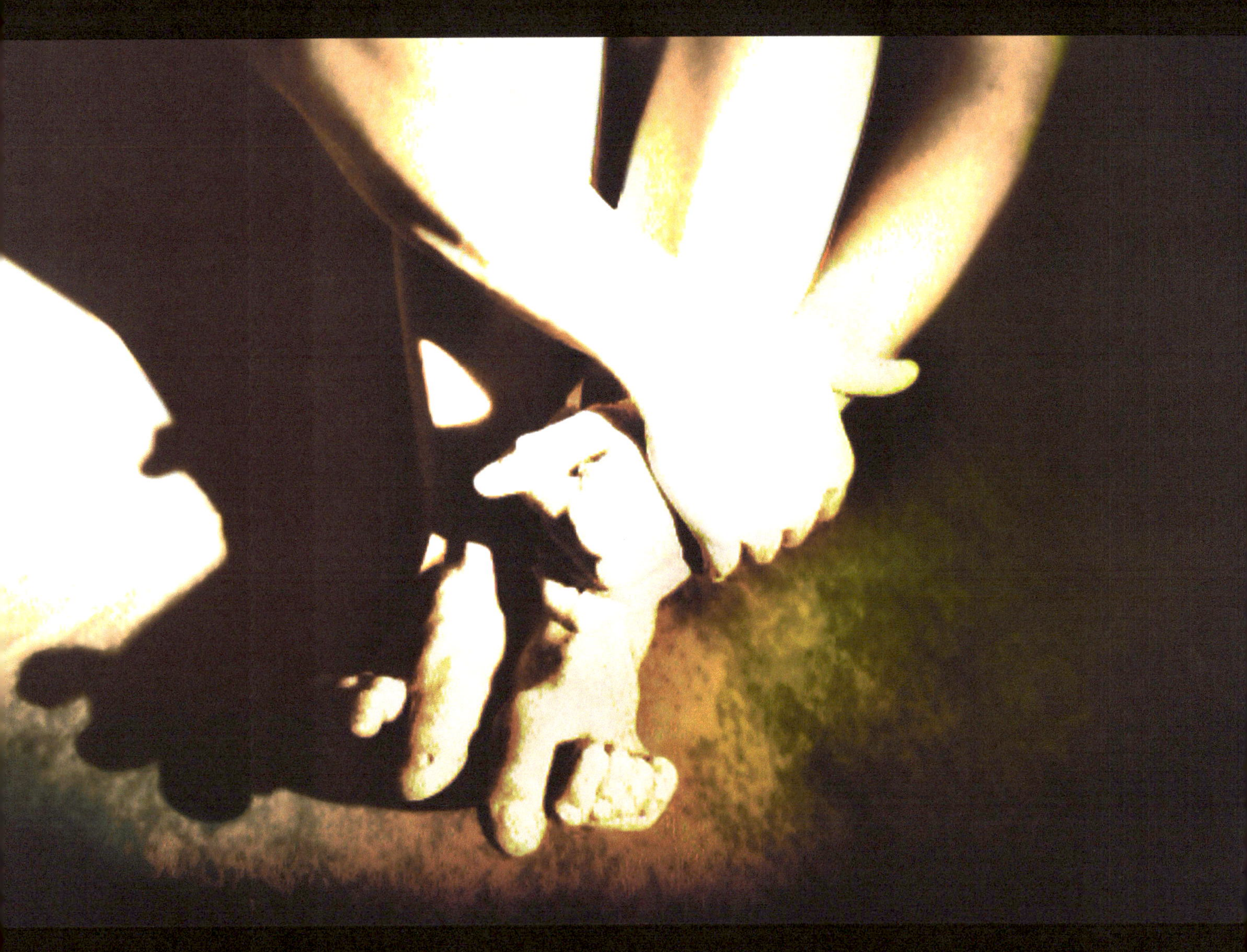

Alexis - pg. 57, 63, 69

Talula - pg. 75, 83, 103

Stephanie "Sunshine" Hite - pg. 79, 81, 107

Carol Schumacher - pg. 85, 89, 95

Ricardo Acevedo - pg. 87, 114, back cover

Jemila Anisa Sunsong - pg. 91

Mona Pitts - pg. 93, 105

Lisa Dean - pg. 109

Sly VanManson - pg. 111

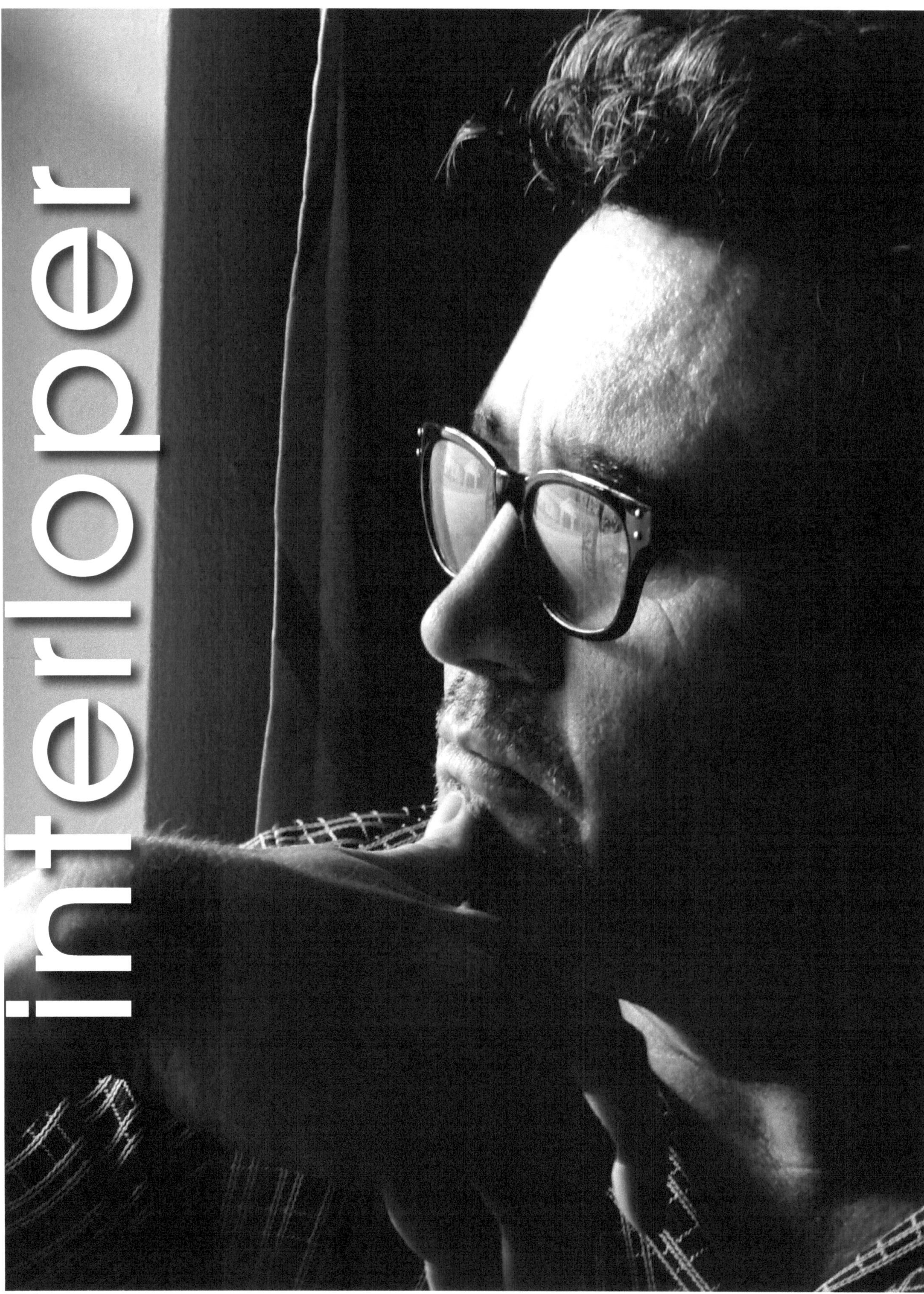

ricardo acevedo

He was born of Yaqui-Mexican & Finn decent. Raised in Southern California, he has pursued artistic endeavors throughout his life. Originally in the visual arts which morphed into music and writing by the 1980's and now has returned full circle...

"Our interactions with others, and our ongoing delving into the different aspects of ourselves. The depth of these mysteries are the things that fascinate me. If only sometimes barely perceptible, our inner and outer variations are almost always most notable in our passions, our physical and spiritual passions.

I consider myself a very passionate creature, and being so, express myself as such. Every form I see is a microcosm. Shadow and light as a painter working the contours and textures. My love of Film Noir and Cinema Fantastic finds its way into all I do and see.

Beyond human inclination, speaking of the condition in all its ugliness and beauty. The places we put ourselves in the search of "IT," the places we end up, letting others define "IT" for us.

My desire is to haunt you with yourself."

~Ricardo Acevedo

[left]
Photograph of the artist
2011 by Violet Spring Acevedo

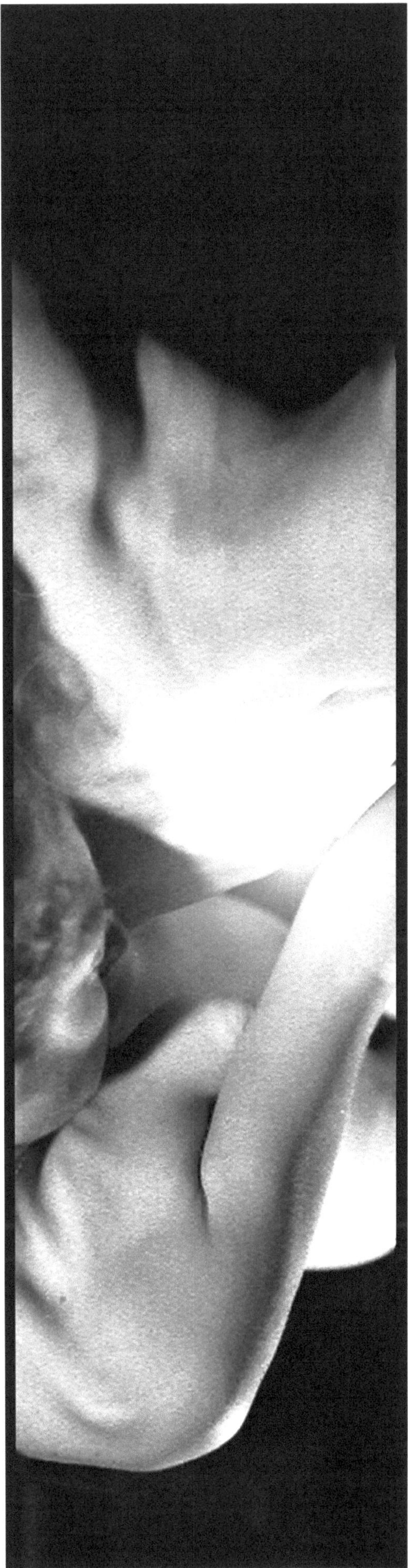

[right]
Horizon
2000 | B/W photo
O.P.S. 12" x 28"

www.ingramcontent.com/pod-product-compliance
Ingram Content Group UK Ltd.
Pitfield, Milton Keynes, MK11 3LW, UK
UKHW060119300726
14090UKWH00002B/272

9780980031270